I0812257

Praise for

No Limits

"Sara Morgan's book is perfect for anyone who has fantasized about becoming self-employed or who has been the victim of layoffs or a dying industry but is afraid to take the first step. No Limits *is incredibly inspirational and authentic and exactly what every would-be entrepreneur needs to read right now to assuage (or ease) their fears and anxiety."*

—**JULIE JANSEN,**

Author of *I Don't Know What I Want, But I Know It's Not This*

"If you've reached your absolute limit in Corporate America then Sara Morgan's No Limits *is the perfect book to take back your life, turn your talents into paydays, and build a sustainable self-employment empire."*

—**JEFF COHEN,**

Author of *The Complete Idiot's Guide to Working Less, Earning More* and President of Boldroad.com, a writing, speaking, and consulting company that inspires people to take action toward working less, earning more, and living a better life through books, products, live seminars, and personalized consulting.

How I Escaped the Clutches of Corporate America to Live the Self-Employed Life of My Dreams

No Limits

Sara Morgan

Custom Solutions
St. Francisville, LA

Custom Solutions

Custom Solutions, LLC
5559 Hilltop Circle
Saint Francisville, LA 70775
http://www.custsolutions.net

Published in the United States of America

Cover and book design by Peri Poloni-Gabriel, Knockout Design, www.knockoutbooks.com

Grateful acknowledgment is made to Free Press for permission to reprint portions of *Chellie's Story* by Marci Shimoff

FIRST EDITION

Library of Congress Cataloging-in-Publication Data is available upon request

ISBN 13: 978-0-615-29932-7

ISBN 10: 0-615-29932-6

Table of Contents

Acknowledgments

To Alex Cook, Annette Pelliccio, Bruce Johnson, Chellie Campbell, Joan Roberts, Mark Dunn and Roger Arrick for doing the interviews and giving me some of the greatest material for this book.

To Stacy, Paul and Sami Morgan for their helpful support and advice.

To Amy Spencer for doing a fantastic job editing the manuscript despite the fact that she had little time to do so.

To Peri Poloni-Gabriel from Knockout Books for her incredible work on the cover and interior design.

To Susan Kendrick from Write To Your Market for her excellent guidance in writing the back cover material.

To Dan Poynter, whom I have not met, but his book The Self-Publishing Manual became like a bible for me.

To Marci Shimoff and Carol Kline for giving me permission to use Chellie's story from Happy for No Reason.

To my Mom and Dad, Bruce and Wendy Morgan, for being most excellent role models. You gave me more love and support than anyone can possibly deserve. I love you both very much.

To my Kids, Christian, Justin and Anna for being the reason for everything I do and the best thing I ever did. I love you.

About the Author

Sara Morgan

SARA MADE THE JUMP TO SELF-EMPLOYMENT in 2005 with the start-up of her consulting company, **Custom Solutions, LLC** (http://www.custsolutions.net). She has always had a keen interest in Artificial Intelligence and Robotics and in 2005 her first book, ***Building Intelligent .NET Applications***, was published. Her long term plans involve using proceeds from this book to fund a project aimed at providing intelligent robotic assistance for the elderly.

She has worked for companies spanning multiple industries, including Health Care, Finance, Retail, Government, and Information Technology. For Microsoft, her primary client for the past few years, she has participated as a Subject Matter expert in the creation of official Microsoft certification exams. She has also co-authored several technical books used to prepare software developers taking the certification exams and even written product documentation for the Office Communications team.

She is an experienced **web developer** with over 15 years of experience developing web sites accessed both internally and over the Internet. Sara is a **Microsoft Certified Developer** and recognized expert in the field of web development using Microsoft SQL Server. She has published six technical books, along with dozens of online and printed articles. In March of 2007 she was awarded the prestigious

Microsoft Most Valued Professional (MVP) award for her work with Microsoft Speech Server and Office Communications Server.

Warning – Disclaimer

THIS BOOK IS DESIGNED to inspire those people seeking self-employment. While the book does provide information about resources a self-employed person can use when starting their business, the information is not exhaustive. Readers seeking to start their own businesses are urged to first read this book and then do additional follow up reading by seeking additional information related to starting and running your own business.

There are many legal and financial issues that must be carefully considered before starting your own business and each business will vary in what these considerations are. While this book does provide information to point you in the right direction, it does not address every consideration that might apply for your unique situation.

The purpose of this book is to educate and entertain. The author and Customs Solutions, LLC shall have neither liability nor responsibility to any person or entity with respect to any loss or damage caused, or alleged to have been caused, directly or indirectly, by the information contained in this book.

If you do not wish to be bound by the above, you may return this book to the publisher for a full refund.

Introduction

Do you really want to wake up one day and regret the fact that you missed a great opportunity when you were younger? I know that I don't, and so I am dedicating the best years of my life towards getting the most out of each day. I firmly believe that each day is a gift that you only get to open once and I strive to end each one with pride and satisfaction.

So why should you listen to me? Because I am where you want to be, and I came from where you are now. I know what it feels like to have a good job that is just not good for you. I know what it is like to feel that despite having worked hard to go to college and acquire a useful skill, you are still not happy with your career and dread going to work. And most importantly, I know what it feels like to overcome these challenges and to find a job that is truly satisfying and meets all my needs.

Whenever I question what is really important in life, I first think of the following quote:

> *"You only live once,*
> *but if you work it right, once is enough."*
>
> Joe E. Lewis (1902 – 1971)

You may be feeling now that despite having followed the rules and done everything everyone told you to, you do not feel satisfied with where you are. You feel like you shouldn't really complain. You may have a nice house, a nice car, a nice family, even a nice dog. But yet something keeps bugging you. Something keeps nagging at you, keeping you up at night and causing you to lose your focus.

What is it? It is you. You are trying to tell yourself that despite having been assured that working hard and following orders would make you happy, it hasn't. You want more. You see more. And quite frankly, you deserve more.

The good news is that it is not too late. There is always a chance to turn things around and to reach for the stars. Your only limitations are the ones you create for yourself. In many ways you are your own worst enemy. Unless you are careful, you may spend the rest of your life waiting for your life to begin.

The last few years, specifically 2008 and 2009, have brought enormous challenges to people all around the world. Not only are there very real and serious world economic problems, but there is a constant threat of terrorism, social unrest, and even pandemics. It would be very easy to allow yourself to be deeply affected by all the negative press and to feel discouraged about yourself and your life. But this is precisely the time when opportunities are the most abundant and your chance of success the highest.

According to the United States Census bureau, about three quarters of all U.S. business firms have no payrolls. They are typically self-employed people flying under the radar, slowly building their reputations and making a real difference in today's economy. The recent recession has simultaneously put a lot of corporate giants out of business, decreasing competition and providing room for small businesses to grow.

More traditional ideas about success and prosperity have become unrealistic and unsustainable, and workers are realizing that we have entered an entirely new economic model in which large and monolithic enterprises are no longer viable. A new model in which small and agile businesses now have the advantage is developing. The new economy insists that successful businesses are able to react quickly and that these businesses are able to closely monitor their markets and rapidly adjust according to their needs.

Now is the time to act. If you have a great idea or a useful skill, you should go for it. Stop waiting for someone to start your life for you. Take control and create your own destiny. I promise you, it will be worth it.

Even if you are not seriously considering a jump to self-employment, you may find value in this book, whose main purpose is to show that it is possible to attain a happy balance between your work and personal life.

In this book, I will tell you how I managed to escape the clutches of corporate America four years ago. Since then, I have written five books, several articles and worked as a software consultant for various companies, including Microsoft- all of this from the comfort of my own home.

At the same time, I have been able to satisfy the ever changing needs of my three young children and become the parent I always wanted to be. The kind of parent that can attend school functions without taking a sick day. The kind of parent that can be home when their kids get off the school bus, and help them with their homework before dinner. The kind of parent that can do all of this and still have time to go running or read a book.

I consider my life so far to be successful. However, if you had asked me ten years ago whether I was happy, I would have told you no. Since then, although I have endured the pain of two failed marriages and tackled the challenge of being a single parent of three children, I am the happiest I have ever been. I am happy because I am able to support my children and be there for them in the way I want to be. I am also able to make a good living doing what I like, the way that I like to do it.

I will begin by telling you how I got to where I am today. But don't worry; this book will not be entirely about me. To prepare for the book, I interviewed a number of people who are self-employed as consultants or own their own business. I have included the profiles of these individuals at the end of each chapter and also incorporated the incredibly useful things they had to say throughout the book.

All of the people I interviewed made a deliberate choice to break out on their own and they have not regretted the decision. The following is a sneak preview of who these people are, along with a special quote from each one:

- **Roger Arrick** – Owner of the Texas-based electronics and robotics company, Arrick Robotics. Roger has been doing his own thing for many years and of all the people interviewed, he has been the most removed from the corporate world. During my interview with him, I asked him what he thought about the idea of corporate security. His response to me was,

  > *"I do fully reject the notion that a large corporation provides security. This is often mentioned as a benefit by my friends who work for one, but they are always talking about how they are sweating*

over the latest round of layoffs. An employee has one customer – their employer. A self-employed person typically has many customers, and losing one of them is survivable."

- **Chellie Campbell** - Creator of the incredibly popular Financial Stress Reduction Workshops and author of *The Wealthy Spirit: Daily Affirmations for Financial Stress Reduction*. Chellie believes that the way we think strongly influences how we do in life. She espouses the idea of repeating daily affirmations to help free yourself from financial stress and make yourself happier at the same time. She had this interesting thing to say,

  "The key factor right now, especially with all the trouble in the economy, is that you have to remain positive and optimistic. Keep an upbeat attitude."

- **Alex Cook** – Independent Software Consultant, freelance music journalist and author of the popular and unpopular music review book, *Darkness, Racket and Twang*. Alex has led many different lives and of all the people profiled, he is the only one who has returned to full-time work at a University after being self-employed for three years. However, the opportunity was one he created for himself and also one that makes him very happy. When asked whether he considered himself to be successful Alex said,

  "I think I am successful. I've come to realize that success is measured by a lot of different rulers, and comparing how happy I am now as compared to when I was a programmer in a corporate setting, working on projects that I didn't necessarily care about, then yes, this has been a huge success."

- **Mark Dunn** – Owner and President of the Atlanta-based software training and consultation firm, Dunn Training and Consultation. Mark is a smart guy with a strong work ethic, who believes that anything is possible as long as you focus on the long term goals rather than the short term profits. He had this to say about building reputations,

> *"Reputations take years to build and minutes to lose. I've heard that many times and believe it. I've always done whatever it takes to deliver for my customers even when it has cost me considerably to finish."*

- **Bruce Johnson** – Partner and Principal Consultant of Toronto-based training and consulting firm, ObjectSharp Consulting. Bruce figured out a long time ago that working in the corporate world was not for him and has been working as a consultant for over seventeen years. When asked about setbacks he has faced in his career he has this to say,

> *"I believe that as an entrepreneur, it's important to be willing to take chances. And, as a mental attitude, the ability to stay calm through the tough times and not let setbacks keep you from making the difficult decisions the next time around."*

- **Annette Pelliccio** – Founder and CEO of the nationwide garden resource network, The Happy Gardener. Annette is a passionate and optimistic person, who found an incredibly unique way to support herself and her family. She had this advice to offer people starting their own businesses,

> *"When venturing out on your own it is very important to have that support from family and friends. Your business is going to impact everyone involved and in order for them to not resent it, they must be aware of the goals and steps needed to make it happen."*

- ✧ **Joan Roberts** – Certified Career Management Coach and Owner of CareerCounseling.com. Joan is more than just a Certified Career Management Coach; she is also a good role model for the self-employed. Since 1992, she has been an independent career coach and she loves the fact that the opportunity allows her to help other people while also being there for her children and family.

> *"Quitting my job in 1992 to pursue my passion of professional career coaching was one of the best things I have ever done. I always say that on my 34th birthday I gave myself the 'gift of freedom'."*

If you are wishing for more out of life, or feel unsatisfied with your current situation and have a great idea, but lack the courage to go forward, then this book is for you. In it, I will tell you the benefits of being on your own and what personal characteristics are needed to make this kind of jump. I will also tell you about the things you need to let go of before embarking on your new journey.

Additionally, I will provide information about important things you need to consider such as taxes, insurance and savings. And finally, I will tell you the things you need to get started, and helpful things to remember as you move forward.

The most important thing you need to succeed and be happy is a willingness to make the effort to make it come true. The fact that you even picked up this book, indicates that you have that willingness. This is not a "how to get rich quick" story. It is a "how do I maximize my potential and feel satisfied and happy with what I am doing in life" story. If that is the kind of story you are looking for, then I encourage you to read further.

Life without a purpose is a
languid, drifting thing; every day
we ought to review our purpose,
saying to ourselves, 'This day let
me make a sound beginning

—Thomas Kempis

Chapter 1

My Story

DESPITE HAVING SKIPPED THE FIRST GRADE, due to my high reading skills, I never really excelled in school. Looking back, I think the reason was more social than anything else; I was a typical teenager, more obsessed with meeting boys and looking cool than doing well in school. Being smart, especially if you were a girl, was not exactly socially enviable. Being labeled a geek was a social death I was sure going to avoid, so for most of my academic career, I just kind of got by. It wasn't until I got into college that I really started to make an effort.

Off to college – Challenge #1

One of my first potential setbacks in college happened at a preliminary screening, which was supposed to match incoming freshmen with appropriate majors. Since I had never worked much in school, my math skills were horrendous. I clearly remember a woman guidance counselor who reviewed my scores and suggested that I not go into anything math related. I, of course, did not listen to a word she said, graduating instead with a degree in Quantitative Business Analysis, with a minor in computer science. That is a fancy way of saying that

I needed to get really good at math, since statistics was the main focus of this major. Computer programming, my other focus, was another skill to which I had no prior exposure before college.

The odds were stacked against me, to say the least. But I pushed forward, determined to make something of myself. Since I had to work full time while attending college, it took me a little longer than four years to graduate – seven years to be exact. Luckily for me, the economy was strong and job opportunities abundant the year I graduated.

The first big job – Challenge #2

At the age of 24 I began my first big job as an Application Analyst for a local hospital. Back then, the mainframe was still the best platform for running large computer applications. I naively thought the two mainframe programming courses I had in college would fully prepare me for the job. Boy was I wrong.

As with most high level skills, the theoretical experience gained in the classroom did not match up with the actual experience required in corporate America. Things were tough for a while, but I held my head high and gradually learned the skills I needed to be successful at my job.

My situation started to improve. I was making good money, although only a fraction of what I currently make, and most importantly I was gaining self-confidence. Three years into this job I had my first experience with how treacherous and cut-throat corporate America can be. It was horrible and I almost lost my hard-won self-confidence completely.

I was privately promised the lead position for a very prominent up-coming project. When the position announcement was made, however, I discovered I would not be the lead as I had been promised.

Although I had been wondering if something was going on behind my back and therefore I was able to quickly recover, my pride had been severely damaged and I knew it was time to move on.

Fortunately, I was able to land an even better job at a large financial services company. I was sure that my experiences at the first company were isolated and would never happen anywhere else.

I approached the new job with renewed optimism and for a while things went well. A few months into my new job, I became pregnant with my first child. The pregnancy went well and at first I planned on only taking 6 weeks of maternity leave. I had no idea that motherhood was going to change me so profoundly.

Motherhood – Challenge #3

Prior to having my first child, my world revolved exclusively around me. Even though I was married, I was still the center of my universe. Parenthood changed that completely.

The planned six weeks turned into twelve weeks and for the first 5 months back to work, I cried every day before going to work. I was wracked with guilt, convinced that I was destroying my child by sending him off to daycare. Of course, I now know that was not true, but I think every new parent goes through this kind of stress.

I made it past my child's first year and shortly after became pregnant with my second child. That pregnancy also went well and by the age of thirty I was married, well employed, and the mother of two beautiful baby boys.

My career was going well and I was acquiring new skills, including web development. I was developing dynamic web sites which accessed data from a database. It was also during this time that I published my first article with the prestigious magazine now recognized as Microsoft Developer Network or MSDN.

So, what could be wrong with this picture? Most people might think, "Nothing!" but something was starting to build inside me. I was restless, unsatisfied, looking for more. I wasn't sure what I was looking for, but I was sure I did not have it. I remember telling people back then that my dream job would be one in which I could just do whatever I wanted and get paid good money for it. Isn't that what we all want?

Unfortunately, the honeymoon with my second job was coming to an end. The huge, publicly traded financial firm employing me hit a bad patch. They had been caught cooking the books, we were told, and their rating hit the floor. In a few short months they went from being one of the biggest employers in Louisiana to bankruptcy. I needed another job.

Short-timer – Challenge #4

Luckily for me, or so I first thought, I quickly landed a job with a local retail company. I would be working for the person who had back-stabbed me in my first job, but I dismissed that as insignificant. I must have been immature back then, I thought. Surely the problem was just with me and my inexperience, and this person would never mislead me again. Wrong. Take it from me – when someone betrays you at work, don't give them a chance to do it again. You will certainly regret it – as did I.

The retail job lasted less than a year – 11 months to be exact. But, I was not going to let that set back ruin me. I immediately landed another job, a much better job. This one would be it, I thought.

Maybe short-term contracting? – Challenge #5

The job was working for a local Application Service Provider (ASP's, they called them back in 2000). I would be the only developer at an all male, all administrative technician based shop. As much as I loved all the guys there, I never quite bonded with this group, which was very unlike me.

But the biggest problem with this job was the fact that I was doing short term contracting work, which is similar to being a fire fighter. You are sent in to quickly put out fires (in this case, software failures) and then get back out. There is nothing proactive about it. People want things done quickly and, most importantly, cheaply.

This type of work has never felt right to me. I like to plan things out and do a good, thorough job. I prefer to be proactive and look for ways to improve the design and make things run more efficiently. Unfortunately, short term contracting clients are not looking for this kind of work, so after two years, I moved on.

A growing desire

During my time as a short-term contractor, I was growing steadily more restless despite my seemingly perfect life. I had earned several Microsoft certifications, which at first made me happy, but later seemed kind of silly. I spent many days and nights pondering what I might do intellectually to satisfy the growing hunger inside me. Additionally, the problems in my first marriage were becoming more obvious.

I had always been interested in the way the brain works. And like a lot of kids growing up in the seventies, I saw Star Wars and became enthralled with R2D2 and C3PO. It seemed like a good idea to combine my existing computer software skills with my interest in the brain and robotics and study the field of Artificial Intelligence.

I first considered going back to school to get a Masters degree. I even went to the local university and spoke to the head of the computer science department about it. I was shocked by how far behind the real world the university was. I was concerned that going back to school would be a step back, not a step forward.

Ultimately, I decided to create my own school, where I was the teacher, student, and Guidance Counselor all rolled into one. I made a deal with my husband that allowed me to spend two nights a week at the library. I spent this time, along with every other free minute I could manage, reading as much as I could about the field of artificial intelligence. The more I read, the more I wanted to know about Artificial Intelligence– an obsession that has continued to this day!

My first book – Challenge #6

Since I knew short term contracting wasn't for me, I thought I might try long term contracting instead. I took a job with a local software development company that designed software solutions for state legislatures. They were creating a new web version of their product and I was able to get in on the project at the beginning.

It was an exciting time for me intellectually. I was doing some really cool web development work during the day and then reading about all sorts of fascinating things at night. In between, I took care of the kids. Unfortunately, this left little time for my marriage, which by now was crumbling fast.

It was at this time that I decided to write a book about artificial intelligence. The book would be targeted towards software developers like me. Initially, I had grand expectations for what would be included but soon discovered that writing a book was a heck of a lot more time-consuming than I thought it would be. The good news is, as with all things in life, the more you write, the better and faster you get at it. However, it was also during this time that I became pregnant with my third child. Things were a bit stressful, to say the least.

Despite all the challenges, I pushed forward and in 2005, after the birth of my daughter, my first book was published: *Building Intelligent .NET Applications.* I was also making really good money at this new job. I later learned that I was being paid almost 20 percent more than the going market rate for my kind of job. The company was willing to pay me and my co-workers extremely well so we would not be tempted to leave them. Times were good, but it wasn't long before my world came crashing down around me.

Towards the end of 2005, the company went through some major changes. The owner of the company, a truly distasteful man who had been hands off up until now, decided he wanted to get more involved in the day to day business. He came through the office like a bull in a china shop, firing people, moving everyone around, and pitting the rest of us against each other. He mistakenly thought that since he was paying me more than the market value, I would be willing to put up with anything.

It was then that I experienced my third back stabbing. A fellow employee and I formed an alliance and I thought we were good friends. She convinced me that we needed to make a stand against the nonsense and that we would quit on the same day.

I was a woman on a mission, and even though I had no other job lined up, I stormed into the office on the agreed-upon day and tendered my resignation. My partner in this plan did not, but she did take the opportunity to negotiate a promotion. Ouch, I did not see that one coming. I have since accepted that there are people in the corporate world who are just looking out for themselves, and unfortunately you need to be very wary of colleagues or bosses who make you big promises. This, however, was a hard pill for me to swallow.

Of course, in time I would realize that the woman actually did me a favor and if not for her, I might have waited too long to start my life again.

Jumping in without a life jacket

So there I was – without a job. I had just a few thousand dollars in savings and my former employer was threatening to sue me if I tried to do contract work for any of my clients. It was sink or swim time.

I decided to use the impetus of the book to start my own consulting business. I borrowed $500 from my mother and set up my own Limited Liability Corporation (LLC) named Custom Solutions, LLC. I had several interviews, but got few call backs. I soon discovered that the rate I was charging was too high. Live and learn! I lowered my rate substantially and managed to land a contract job with a local financial firm. The work was not very exciting, but the paycheck was steady and came just at the right time.

During the day I worked at my consulting job and at night I began co-authoring technical books for Microsoft. The books would be used by software professionals to study for Microsoft certification exams. The work was hard and the hours unreasonable. I had little time for sleep or anything else and knew if I kept up the pace, I would eventually go crazy. To add to the stress, my marriage had officially fallen apart and in early 2006 I asked my husband for a divorce.

After a few months of the non-stop work, I was able to stop the contract job and just focus on writing books for Microsoft full time. At the same time I began email correspondence with the man who would become my second husband. Unfortunately, I had little time left for my kids, which I now regret more than anything.

I have since realized that my situation was difficult because I jumped into the contract world without a life jacket (as in a savings account). I also jumped without a plan and at a time when my personal life was in tatters. Although this may not have been the ideal situation, I did recover and -believe it or not- this does have a happy ending!

The job of writing books for Microsoft, while enjoyable, was not all that financially appealing. I am a bit of a perfectionist and therefore took great pains to make sure I got everything right. I could have taken shortcuts, but I am just not that type of person. As an example of the problem, for one of the books, I estimated that I made a little over $15.00/hour when you include all the time spent in edits and re-edits. I could have made much more money working as a consultant, and I certainly could have done better working as a full-time employee. As much as I liked writing the books, I had to make a change.

Moving to the country

While all this was going on, I divorced my first husband and was actively dating my soon-to-be second husband. I had also moved with my kids from Baton Rouge, the state capitol of Louisiana, to a rural area a few miles north.

Saint Francisville is a small and picturesque town, home to historic plantations and beautiful antique stores. It is the picture of small town American life, a place where my kids can ride their bikes all afternoon and play for hours in our wooded backyard. There could not be a better, safer place for kids to grow up in. Since I work from my home and satellite gets me the internet access I need to work, I can live in a beautiful place like this and still support my children.

The move to Saint Francisville was a big and positive change for me. Not only did it give me a great place to raise my children, but moving allowed me to drastically reduce my expenses. The public school system in Baton Rouge is not very good and consequently many parents send their children to private institutions instead. Private schools cost almost as much as college these days. The monthly cost for three children going to a modestly priced private school in Baton Rouge is well over $1600/month. By moving to Saint Francisville and enrolling my children in the public, highly-ranked school system, I have saved enough money to pay my entire monthly mortgage cost, which at this point is my primary expense. You can see how this move was worth it!

Living in a rural area is a much simpler form of life. Over time that simplicity, along with other changes I was making in my life, helped to create a strong sense of inner peace for me. It also gave me a greater clarity, which made decisions much easier to make.

During our first two years in Saint Francisville, I continued working as an independent contractor and technical writer. I had a few clients for whom I did programming work, one of them was a small robotics company named Coroware and another was a healthcare information consulting company named Health Data Specialists. I also did some technical writing for one of the groups at Microsoft, producing documentation to support one of their products. Documentation turns out to be much more lucrative than writing certification books. The deadlines are also much more reasonable. I was really hitting my stride with work and finally seeing the fruits of my labor pay off. I was also getting a chance to really be there for my children every day, which was very important to me.

My second husband, who is from England, is also a software developer. Unlike most developers, he specializes in Artificial Life and Artificial Intelligence. I guess you can see why I was so attracted to him. We married in 2008 and shortly after decided to start our own business in which he would build robots that we could then rent to companies to advertise their products at conferences. I would help out with the speech aspect of the robot, since that was an area that I had previously specialized in. The fact that we both worked from home allowed us to really minimize expenses. Things were perfect – I finally had the job of my dreams and I was living in my personal version of paradise.

A new beginning

Unfortunately, my second marriage did not last long. My second husband and I separated in the early spring of 2009. As you can imagine, I was devastated. Since I was not expected to be at a job every day and therefore had the freedom to take a little time for myself, I spent the first three weeks searching my soul for answers. In the end I realized that despite the fact that the second marriage had failed, I was still living in paradise and I still had the job of my dreams, so things were really still good. I doubt my response would have been so positive without this particular working situation.

I decided to start writing this book based on an "aha" moment that occurred to me during all that soul searching. I read the negative news headlines and hear about all the challenges facing people these days. These challenges can be especially acute for hard-working parents, like me. I want to tell all these people that there is still hope and that if you want more from life and are willing to work hard and think creatively, it is possible to be happy. I know that I am happy and I hope that this book inspires other people to reach for the stars and realize that there really are no limits.

A note about being a woman in the Information Technology world

Even though I have been described as a feminist, I neither dislike men nor mind working with them. I do, however, think that there needs to be more women in the Information Technology world. Currently, women make up only a small fraction of the work force in this area. According to a study by the National Science Foundation, the percentage of females employed in mathematical or computer science jobs decreased from 31 percent in 1983 to 25 percent in 2007. Many people have various theories on why this is the case.

Software development is a very competitive field. Programmers are always subject to code reviews, in which fellow employees or students are given the opportunity to examine the code and provide feedback. This can be quite intimidating. It certainly is for me! Additionally, the math and science requirements for this profession can put some people off.

I personally believe the reason more women do not enter this field is that they are intimidated. My hope is that if girls see successful, happy women in this business, then more of them would want to enter the field. I hope this book is read by a young woman considering entering the field of software development and it inspires her to push past the intimidation and not give up.

After being in this business for over 15 years, I cannot imagine doing anything else that would give me the same kind of satisfaction, nor allow me the same kinds of opportunities for success. I hope other young women can join me in reaping some of these benefits.

And in the end
it's not the years in your life
that count.
It's the life in your years.

—Abraham Lincoln

Chapter 2:

What Are the Benefits?

When I asked the people I interviewed about the benefits of being self-employed, they all quickly responded with something truly wonderful to say. Each of them has benefited tremendously from working for themselves, as have I. In this chapter, I will share some of my experiences, along with their responses.

Casual dress, all the time

Corporate offices have long known that people prefer casual dress to formal business attire. It is just more comfortable and the clothes are considerably cheaper. For this reason, many of the offices I worked in over the years allowed employees to dress "business casual", which meant no ties and suits for the men and no hose and dress suits for women.

While that was nice and it certainly helped to reduce my dry cleaning expenses, business casual for me now means staying in my bathrobe until noon if I want to. I can also wear shorts in the summer, which seems almost critical for anyone living in the Deep South. Only occasionally do I meet with a client and on those occasions I usually dress in what would be considered business casual. It is on those days that I realize business casual is really not casual at all.

Profile: My work environment

To give you a better idea of what my life is like now, I wanted to show you a few pictures of my home office and current work environment. The majority of what I consider to be my office space is actually outside, since I just prefer being outdoors.

My primary desk is located inside my bedroom. Since I deal with computers and most of my work is digital, I do not require a large work space. I therefore selected a small and simple space to help maintain a sense of order.

The areas that I am most proud of are the places I go during the day when I take breaks. I personally work best when I take frequent breaks, so I have set up several areas around my house where I can go to unwind and think. I call them my break rooms.

The first break room is located just outside my bedroom window. This is where I eat my lunch every day, and on days when the work load is light and the sun is bright, I spend a few minutes after lunch lying in the sun. Oh, and in case you are wondering, that is a white bunny rabbit in the picture. Her name is Riley.

The next break room is where I usually go in the afternoon. You can't see it in this picture, but the sky view from those chairs is amazing. It is a very peaceful place to sit and relax.

The last break room is a spot overlooking a large ravine in my back yard. This picture was taken at the first of spring when the woods were covered with beautiful green foliage.

And finally, when the day is nice and I just don't feel like working inside, I move to my outside desk. I ran an outdoor power cable to this patio table and because I have a strong wireless network, my laptop works perfectly outside. I try not to work here too much, since the chair and table are not ergonomically correct.

Truly flexible work hours

Flexible work hours are another perk most companies now offer. I was personally able to take advantage of this at only two of the companies I worked for. I thought I was an early bird and also, since I have kids, it was better for me to come in early and leave early. A typical work day is 8am to 5pm, but the companies I worked for allowed me to shift that to a 7am to 4pm or 6am to 3pm time frame. While this was helpful, it was only flexible to a point.

In this self-employment process I have discovered that I actually work best in the afternoons and late evenings. I don't know why, but it seems that my brain is more efficient and I am the most creative at those times. For this reason, I typically spend my mornings taking care of housework and any other business. I then work in the afternoons and take a long break when the kids get home from school. I am able to help them with their homework and fix a nice dinner before returning to work in the later evening.

This kind of schedule seems to work best for me and I feel that I get more accomplished now than I ever did working at a full time job. I realize that an employer would have a hard time extending this kind of flexibility because it would be too hard to manage. Being self-employed, I only have to worry about managing myself, so there is no problem.

Having flexible hours also means you can spend more time doing what is most important to you. As Alex Cook puts it, "The greatest benefit to being self employed is that you can contour your work life to fit your non-work life in a much more organic manner. Unless you are directly and regularly interfacing with customers, your hours are yours to set. During the time I worked for myself, I never missed an important moment with my daughter because I was in yet another pointless meeting, or staring at the clock on my monitor, and for me that was huge."

Roger Arrick agrees with Alex and said, "The greatest single thing about working for myself is the schedule. I can work when I have energy and inspiration, and rest or do personal errands as needed. What really matters is what I accomplish, not how many hours I pull. I'm somewhat embarrassed to admit this schedule includes getting up at 8am, taking a short nap in the afternoon, and maybe working till 11pm."

Able to enjoy a hobby

Like most people, as middle age started to approach I realized that I could not eat nearly as much as I used to without gaining a lot of weight. Around the age of 36 I took up running. At first it was nearly impossible and the first time I went out running (if you can even call it that), I only got half a block before feeling like my lungs were on fire.

I hung in there and every time I went out, I was able to get a little further down the road before I stopped to walk. Two years later I ran my first marathon and it was the best thing I ever did. I do not run marathons any more, but I would never have been able to run the first one if I had not been self-employed at the time. To train for a marathon you need to build until you are running up to 30 miles a week. I could never have done that while working a full time job.

The benefits I get from running are more than just the improved fitness and ability to eat more. Every time I run, I gain confidence and feel empowered. I am also able to think very clearly and some of my best ideas have occurred to me while out on a run.

I am not saying that everyone should take up running, although I do encourage it. Whatever your hobby, be it golf, fishing, or tennis, being self-employed will allow you to enjoy it more fully.

No office politics

I am a big fan of the NBC show, *The Office*. I tune in every week to see what crazy things the boss Michael is doing that week. I am never disappointed and the show always offers a good laugh. The show is funny because the office politics seen on that show occur in most real offices all the time, although usually not quite as exaggerated.

Most viewers can identify at least one character on the show with a person they used to work with, or work with now. While funny on the show, I doubt most people find it funny in their real lives. For me, the absence of office politics is one of the top benefits of being self-employed.

Gain a sense of accomplishment

I think back on my work experiences and remember many days when I felt that I was getting nowhere and accomplishing nothing. I felt guilty about that, as if I was robbing my employer of the pay I was receiving. I now realize that I was simply not challenged enough by my job, and have learned that when I am properly motivated, I am able to accomplish almost anything. The sense of accomplishment I get from my job now is huge, and it gives me a wonderful feeling of pride and satisfaction that I never felt as a corporate employee.

Annette Pelliccio, who is profiled at the end of this chapter agrees, and had this to say, "The greatest benefit to being self-employed is stepping back, looking at what you have created and seeing how it has evolved as a result of all of the unshaken dedication, persistence and care."

Work the way you work best

As individuals we all have different styles and methods of working. For example, I work best when I am able to take frequent breaks, as in at least one per hour. I do not need a long one, but I need enough time to get up from the desk, walk around and do something other than my job.

When I used to work in the corporate world, these breaks often involved going to the bathroom or the vending machine in the break room. If I felt pressed to find something legitimate, I would look for a reason to go see a coworker or the boss. Although none of my ex employers ever formally complained about my constant moving around, I caught enough eye rolls and heavy sighs to know that many were not happy about it.

These days when I feel the need to take one of these breaks, I go load some laundry or quickly wash the dishes. Sometimes, I just go outside to one of many break rooms and sit to think. I no longer have to worry about the repercussions of my wandering ways. In the end, I know that I always get the job done and the more freedom I have, the more efficient and the higher quality my work is.

I am not alone in that I thrive in this type of atypical work pattern. While doing the interviews for this book, I discovered that Roger Arrick also makes it a point to regularly seek a change of scenery. In one of his responses, he stated that, "One issue I have to consciously work on is to pace myself. I'm driven but can get worn down if I don't watch out. I almost never do anything for more than an hour. I need a change of scenery and focus regularly. When I hit a problem that seems impossible, I usually stop and let the day pass".

Another person who thrives in a less controlled environment is Alex Cook. He said, "Your work location is fluid - I remember one day where I worked in a client's office, a coffee shop and on the bank of the river all in a single day. The grind aspects of work fade away; when you don't feel like working, you can put it aside and do something else, provided you actually pick it back up later."

When you are self-employed, you have the freedom to work whatever way works best for you. For some that might mean sitting down at the desk, focusing really hard for 4 to 6 hours and then taking the rest of the day off. Others might find they work best when the television is running (something I doubt most employers would approve of). Whatever method or technique you have for being efficient is ok when you are self-employed.

Bruce Johnson had this to say about the freedom of self-employment, "One of the things I still love almost twenty years after starting on this path is the freedom it gives me. While it's not quite completely true, I do have the ability to take or turn down any gig I get offered. On a day-to-day basis, I can decide if I want to go to work or not. I can start earlier or later and end at the corresponding time as the other aspects of my life demand."

Exactly what benefits a person gets from being self-employed will vary from person to person and may even vary for the same person over time. For example, when asked about the greatest benefit to being self-employed, Mark Dunn said, "When I was younger, I would have said the single greatest benefit is the ability to make the decisions that drive the business for better or worse. Now, I think the greatest benefit is being able to help others as a mentor so they don't have to repeat the same mistakes I've made in the past. Having time to invest in other people is a huge dividend."

In this next profile, you will learn about a truly inspirational single mother of two who took a childhood passion and turned it into a money making business.

Annette Pelliccio — Founder and CEO of The Happy Gardener

Even though we have vastly different career choices, I related to Annette Pelliccio the most of all the people I interviewed. Annette, like me, is a single mom who has invented her own career in order to support her kids financially and also be there when they need her. She earned an undergraduate degree in Special Education and a Masters degree in Curriculum and Instruction, with a concentration in reading. But education was not the career path that Annette would pursue after her children were born.

> *"Do what you are completely passionate about. In order to succeed and be truly happy, you must love what you do"*

Initially, Annette opted to be a stay-at-home mom, but after her second child was born, she felt the desire to return to work. Even though she desired a career that would satisfy her personal development, she knew that a conventional job would not allow her the flexibility she needed for her kids. Her solution was to take a huge risk and start her own business based on a long held family passion – gardening.

As a concerned parent, Annette was worried about the chemical pesticides being used in the food she fed her children. She also saw the negative effects that chemical fertilizers were having on the environment. Independently, she had been researching her own line of organic products to use with her family and this led her to the decision to blend her passion for organic gardening with a home-based business.

In 2003, Annette borrowed $3000 from her family and launched The Happy Gardener, Inc, (http://www.thehappygardener.info) a direct seller of organic products which is also committed to educating people about earth friendly garden and lawn care practices. It was slow going at first and even though she had many sleepless nights and little free time, she used her love of people to create relationships with successful mentors who helped guide her through the rough times. The result is that in 2007, Forbes.com selected The Happy Gardener as one of twenty finalists for their "Boost your Business Contest".

Like me, Annette suffered the financial and emotional turmoil caused by divorce. Rather than giving up, she used the financial need to give her the necessary push to work even harder at making her company successful. She now considers herself a balanced person, who is able to "make sure my family (especially my children), friends, spiritual life and recreational life are not neglected."

Annette is also able to provide a community service that she is very proud of and passionate about. As her website states, The Happy Gardener is "Doing what's right for the environment, our families, the community, home gardeners, and for our future".

I believe the most successful type of person in the world of self-employment is someone with a strong sense of self. Successful entrepreneurs tend to be the kind of people that never quite fit in with the establishment and always seem to follow their own path. They are also the ones that select an area of business about which they are very passionate. Passion is a powerful emotion and an excellent motivator, capable of navigating someone through the occasionally challenging waters of self-employment.

Anyone who thinks
the sky is the limit,
has limited imagination.

— Anonymous

Chapter 3:

What Type of Person Do You Need to Be?

JOAN ROBERTS IS A CERTIFIED CAREER MANAGEMENT COACH and owner of CareerCounseling.com. She told me, "I coach many clients who are dissatisfied with their employment situations. It could be that they want a better boss, more money or more satisfaction from their work. Many of those clients will simply change jobs. However, the clients who no longer feel passion in their work or are searching for more meaning in their work lives are typically go-getters. They have achieved exactly what they have set out to achieve, but something is still missing. They want more meaning and purpose in their lives. They want to make an impact and feel drawn to being in charge of their own destinies. This leads them down the path of self-employment and a future that is solely in their hands."

Self-employment, whether it is as a consultant or a business owner, is certainly not for everyone. In this chapter, I will examine traits that can increase the odds of self-employment success, as these traits are useful tools for overcoming the stresses and challenges associated with self-employment. It is not necessary to possess all of these traits at the outset to be successful; some of these traits may develop over time and others not at all. If, however, you think that *none* of the traits describe you, then you may want to reconsider the jump to self-employment as you may find self-employment to be extremely difficult. Even though self-employment offers many benefits, it is also often stressful and full of challenges. Bruce Johnson, who is a Partner with ObjectSharp Consulting, had this to say, "Some people don't like the insecurity of the life as a consultant. That's something you need to honestly ask yourself (and answer) before you dip a toe into the self-employment pool."

However, if you are the type of person that already possesses all of these traits, what are you waiting for? Self-employment could certainly be your thing. So get out there and do it. Even if you possess all these skills but are not considering self-employment, then congratulations! You should be able to capitalize on these traits to make your life in the corporate world easier.

Strong and Independent

I used the words strong and independent together because being an independent thinker often requires a high-level of inner strength and resolve. These qualities are especially critical when you first make the jump to self-employment.

If you constantly require validation in order to feel you are doing a good job, you may find the move to self-employment particularly stressful. It is likely that in the initial days and months of your business, you will receive little or no feedback. You must be able to continue on your chosen path despite the lack of feedback, confident that you have made the right choice and that you are acting appropriately.

This is especially true for me as I write the manuscript for this book. I have made the decision to self-publish this book despite the fact that my previous six books were all done with a publisher. This requires me to assume all the tasks previously taken care of by my publisher-which is a great many things, I must say! Instead of just writing a book and then approving a few edits, I now have to coordinate peer reviews and manage the long list of people that comprise the book industry. This includes hiring consultants, book cover designers, editors, and printing companies. It includes working with wholesale book distributors and the never ending job of book promotion. Trust me; it is not an easy undertaking.

So why do it? One reason, primarily: I knew that the material in this book was timely and that it needed to get in the hands of readers as soon as possible. The only way I could see to make that possible was to self-publish. I have been through the book proposal process enough times to know that publication does not happen quickly, and so, despite the huge amount of effort required, I needed to have the strength to not only write this book, but to also take on the challenge of self-publishing.

As you can guess, strength and independence are traits I exhibit. While it is not necessary for you to have the strength needed to take on the task of self-publishing, it is necessary for you to have the strength to make your own decisions and enough confidence about those decisions to persevere.

Finisher

This is one of those traits which people may claim they have, but in reality, they do not. You have to be really honest with yourself when thinking about whether you are a finisher. We all have a tendency to blame other people when things do not go our way. For example, someone might say, "it was my bosses' fault that the project I started was cancelled." While in some cases this can be true, I have found that frequently projects are cancelled because the person was taking too long, going in the wrong direction, or spending too much money.

If you review your past accomplishments and see many projects that were started with the best of intentions but were never completed, then self-employment may not be the best area for you. When you are self-employed, your errors cannot simply be brushed under the table or offset by other projects. If a self-employed person fails to finish even one project, it could be the difference between success and bankruptcy.

As Roger Arrick puts it, "Once I decide on a goal, that's most of what I think about until it's done. I always finish projects, even if there is no reason to do so, because I am scared of developing a habit of not finishing."

Even if you have not been employed long enough to rack up a pile of successful projects, you can still look at projects you have started in your personal life. For example, did you ever finish that fence you started to build, or that scrapbook you wanted to put together? Did you finish college or that special training class you signed up for? If you can make a list of *completed* projects, then you are probably a finisher.

Multitasking

The ability to successfully multitask is more an art than a science. Being able to juggle several tasks at once does not necessarily mean you will be able to handle those tasks well. Some people can manage several things at one time, but when the number of things to manage grows too quickly, a person can become overwhelmed and over time this leads them to feel like nothing is being accomplished.

Roger Arrick, states, "I am a multi-tasker, but I have to manage that very closely or the work to accomplishment ratio will get off and I'll feel like I'm not getting anywhere." Roger shared with me his method of managing this work to accomplishment ratio. "I need accomplishments to feed my sense of well being and provide ambition to do the next one. Normally, I have one or two home projects. For the most part, I focus on one major home project and one major work project at any given time."

I too have often found it difficult to manage the many things that life and work throws at me. I believe that the ability to successfully multitask is a skill that can be developed over time. Even if you cannot handle several things at once now, you can set small, achievable goals that will give you a greater sense of accomplishment and improve your ability to manage multiple tasks.

Bruce Johnson had this to say about multi-tasking, "Because I 'm a partner in a consulting company, there are inevitable interruptions over the course of the day. It is a rare occurrence when I can sit down and spend 8 hours straight on a single task. Instead, I usually find myself pulled in different directions based on the incoming requests from consultants, sales people and administrators. My personality is such that I actually revel in that situation. I have developed, over the years of training, the ability to swap in and out of tasks very quickly, a skill that serves me in good stead now."

It is likely that a jump to self-employment will increase the number of things you have to manage. It is a good idea to recognize early on that you need to find clever ways to balance all the things expected of you.

Disciplined

Taking multi-tasking a step further, not only is it important that you are able to handle many things, but that you are able to handle them well. The ability to act efficiently is critical for the self-employed person. This is especially true in the initial days and months when you may have few or no employees to help you. As a result, you must be disciplined and self-motivated.

This does not necessarily mean you have to be a "neat freak" or someone that is overly organized. "I am a balanced person – to do that I am disciplined. I would not consider myself a neat/organized person," says Annette Pelliccio.

Like Annette, I would not consider myself to be overly neat or organized. I certainly know other people who have much cleaner houses and more organized lives. I routinely forget peoples' birthdays or even snack day at my children's school. What I do have, is the discipline to focus on a single task and follow it through to completion, even if doing so makes me uncomfortable. I believe it is this ability to zero in on and complete a project that is so important for a self-employed person.

Creative

It may be necessary for you to really think outside the box when coming up with an innovative idea or product. The business you start may not be in an established business segment or easily definable. You may have to stretch your imagination and step outside your normal comfort zone in order to see what will work best for you.

Once you get the business established, your creativity is crucial in order to make your business stand out from the others. Annette Pelliccio says, "I am absolutely the creative energy behind my company." Through The Happy Gardener, Annette has brought to market some incredibly unique and innovative products, such as SeaResults for Cut Flowers, which Annette says, "is an organic certified, cut flower preservative that is safe for children and pets and prolongs the flower bloom time. It is also packaged in post-consumed recycled cardboard so it is eco-friendly and toxin-free."

Another innovative and creative thinker is Roger Arrick, who states, "I am very creative and am good at coming up with ideas that are outside the box. I think the main reason for that is that I have no formal training that tells me how to do things. Plus I get a charge out of doing things differently and coming up with something unique. It's very discouraging for me to have an idea and find out that someone else in another place and time did the same thing."

Risk Taker

In order to get to where you want to be in life, you must be willing to do something different and take some risks. "If what you're doing now was enough, you'd already be where you want to go," says Chellie Campbell, author of *The Wealthy Spirit*. But if you're reading this book, then what you're doing now is probably not enough.

Risk tolerance varies greatly from person to person. At one extreme are people who can tolerate little or no risk at all. Such people shun any activities that are volatile or unpredictable. At the other extreme are people who crave risk and say yes to absolutely everything. Neither of these types would do well in the world of self-employment. Somewhere in the middle is more preferable.

You must be able to accept a certain amount of risk when making the venture into self-employment. Let's face it, self-employment is a risk. But I firmly believe that if you do something that you like and are passionate about, your chances of success go up dramatically. Unless you are willing to assume some amount of risk in your life, you may never reap the benefits you so richly deserve.

Optimistic

Numerous studies have shown that optimistic people lead happier, healthier, and more productive lives. According to a recent study by the Mayo Clinic, they also have better coping skills during hardships and times of stress. This approach to life and its benefits may be critical for someone entering the world of self-employment.

Are you the type of person who sees the glass as half full or half empty? Remember, you need to be truthful with yourself here. I can remember a time when I would have thought of myself as an optimist, when in fact I was really a pessimist. I realized this when I ran into a former work friend one day at lunch. I happened to be having a particularly good day and so when my friend asked me how things were going, I went on and on about all the fantastic things that were happening and what I was expecting for the future. My friend was visibly surprised by all my good news and jokingly told me they never thought of me as an optimist.

Initially I was shocked by my friend's comment, but soon I realized that the comment was true. I was a pessimist. Most of my thoughts were negative and this resulted in my saying and doing many negative things. It was at that point that I made a deliberate choice to turn things around and start thinking more positively. This is just one of many changes I have made in the past few years that have resulted in a more fulfilling life.

The good news is that even if you are not a naturally optimistic person, it is not too late to improve your outlook on life. Doing so will not only help you succeed in your business ventures, but will also make you happier. I know that the positive steps I have taken in the past few years have led me towards a more fulfilling life, both personally and professionally. I believe everyone has the potential to make the same kinds of steps towards fulfillment in their lives.

Mark Dunn – Owner and President of DUNN Training and Consulting

I have to tell you something about Mark Dunn that I think speaks volumes about the kind of person he is. When I sent out questions to the people I interviewed for this book, Mark was the first to respond. Not only did he respond within a day, but his answers were some of the most thorough and insightful ones I received.

Mark has been "slinging code," as he puts it, for most of his life. He graduated from college with a double major in Mathematics and Physics, but Mark is more a self-taught man. After graduating, he taught himself programming by reading a book, and learned enough to land his first job as a COBOL programmer. Since then, he has become certified with Oracle and other technology products, including those offered by Microsoft.

For the first three years after college, he took many low paying jobs in order to build up his resume with real world skills. "I worked really long hours during that time and was constantly trying to pick up new techniques and learn anything I could from other programmers around me. Looking back, it would have been easier if I'd pursued a computer science degree. It's hard to know what you are going to be when you first declare a major. I sacrificed a lot of time with my family early on," Mark says.

> *"I'm grateful to live in a country where anyone can hang out a shingle, start a business and achieve their dreams."*

In 2002, Mark started his own company, DUNN Training and Consulting (http://dunntraining.com). The Atlanta-based business provides technical training and software consulting services for customers and individuals wanting to utilize Microsoft technologies. Mark is responsible for managing a team of consultants, as well as five full-time employees. Even though his business has grown substantially since it began in 2002, Mark says that, "If success means owning a jet and four homes, then I'll probably never get there. I've never really cared about the lifestyles of the rich and famous. I'm happy to pour my efforts into making others that work with me successful today."

When asked whether he considered himself to be happy, Mark insists that he is very happy and even though he still has to travel, his daily commute is just the walk from the kitchen to his basement office. He has more time to spend with his family, and he says, "…as my kids have gotten older that has been a true blessing for me."

Each of these discussed traits will help ease someone's journey through self-employment – but they are certainly not requirements. These traits I've discussed are just starting points and many of them you may develop over time. For example, when asked whether he exhibited these all of traits when he began his business, Mark Dunn, who initially struggled with the art of multi-tasking, responded, "All the attributes in your list are desirable to be successful in any career. I'm living proof that if you don't possess them in your youth they can be developed". Mark suggests that people make a list of their strengths and weaknesses and then set achievable yearly goals designed to improve those weaknesses.

What is most important to your success is that you have the drive and desire to reach for something better, and are willing to adjust your work habits and outlook on life to achieve your goals.

There is nothing as remarkable as learning how to think better.

—Anonymous

Chapter 4:

Letting Go

SOMETIMES WE MUST TAKE A STEP BACKWARDS before we can take a step forward. In my experience, the path to self-employment has involved letting go of many things; in some cases these were relationships or physical possessions, and in other cases it involved changing how I looked at the world.

In this chapter I will go through each of the things that were most important for me to let go of. By evaluating and prioritizing these things I was able to once again move forward with confidence; sure that I was making the right choices for me and my family.

Let go of blame

You have probably heard the phrase "the blame game". The mainstream media love to play this game in the aftermath of some catastrophe. Whether it is a natural disaster like Hurricane Katrina or a man-made disaster like the 2008 financial meltdown on Wall Street, someone involved in the event is usually quick to stand up and point a finger at someone else.

The blame game rarely has any discernable winner and does not result in a feeling that justice was served or the truth unveiled. Assigning blame, regardless of people's intentions, is generally futile. This is especially true when we blame other people for things that happen to us. Every time we blame someone else for something that happened to us, we miss an opportunity to honestly evaluate our role in what occurred. We miss the opportunity to learn from our mistakes and find new ways to solve our problems. We get caught up in playing the role of the victim and not the victor.

In the world of self-employment, the margin for error can be very small, since your customer base may be highly intolerant of mistakes or delays in service If you continually find someone else to blame when a problem occurs, you may soon find that all fingers are pointing back to you, which can have a disastrous consequence on your professional life.

Chellie Campbell, who is profiled at the end of this chapter, knows all too well how destructive the assignment of blame can be. Her fiancé ended their relationship three weeks before their wedding and to top it off, he married someone else ten weeks later. Ouch. At first, Chellie willingly played the part of the victim and wallowed in her sorrow for far too long. Rather than accepting her responsibility for dismissing the obvious warning signs her fiancé had been exhibiting for months, she chose to focus on blaming everyone else. The anger sat on her like a ton of bricks.

Fortunately for her, Chellie was able to see how destructive her feelings were and eventually she was able to let go of the blame and focus on living her life again. As she said, "I wanted to be a winner, but I couldn't do it by making him a loser. I had to stop thinking like a victim, stop blaming other people for my misfortunes, stop telling victim stories".

Once she did this, Chellie quickly recovered and was able to build her business to the point that she started teaching a series of very popular Financial Stress Reduction workshops. This opportunity led her to write two popular books, "The Wealthy Spirit" and "Zero to Zillionaire". She is now a very happy and balanced person who strives to help others become winners too. As she said, "Blaming is a no-win proposition and I've got better things to do—like being peaceful, content, and happy."

Let go of the fear of failure

We all have fears, some of which serve to protect us from danger and keep us safe. But some fears, like the fear of failure, prevent us from trying new things. Until you can let go of the fear of failure you will be unable to truly succeed.

Letting go of this fear is especially important for the self-employed person. I realize that fifty percent of new businesses fail in the first year, but if you get caught up in worrying about statistics you will never be one of the fifty percent that succeed. Yes, that's right; fifty percent of the people that start a new business do well and actually thrive. Instead of thinking of the ones that fail, focus on the ones that succeed.

Let go of people that limit and restrict you

This is a tough one, but a very necessary step nonetheless. Not everyone in your life is good for you. It is possible that someone close to you will be holding you back in life. These people are not bad people. They are usually just selfish people who cannot see that they are projecting their own fear of failure upon you. They are not deliberately trying to hurt you, but regardless of their intentions if they prevent you from taking charge and moving forward with your life, then they are hurting you.

It is usually easy to figure out who these people are when you start paying attention. To determine who might be limiting you, really listen to conversations you have with relatives, friends, coworkers or even neighbors over the next few days. When speaking with each person, mention something that you would like to try that is very different from your usual habits. It can be something simple, such as eating at a brand new restaurant; notice which of these people try to discourage you from doing something new.

Remember, these people are not bad and they probably have no idea that their negative attitudes are preventing you from trying new things, but they are holding you back and you need to be aware of it. It is not necessary for you to let go of these people entirely and have no contact with them. Some of these people may be your family and you simply cannot abandon a family member, no matter how negative they are.

You do need to recognize that they are influencing your decisions and that you need to take steps to prevent their attitude from affecting you. Whether this means simply reminding yourself to ignore their objections or physically distancing yourself depends on your particular situation. Only you can decide what is right.

Let go of other people's expectations of you

When you read this title, you may have thought I was referring to parent's expectations for their children. And yes, while parent's expectations are a very strong influence on most people's lives, typically these expectations are not damaging. Most parents just want their kids to be happy. Even though some parents may hope their children turn out to be doctors or even movie stars, in the end all they really want is for their child to be satisfied with their life.

The expectations that often derail us from our goals are the social expectations that we all feel the need to fulfill. I know that when I first became a mother, I instantly felt like I was under some kind of spotlight. I assumed everyone was judging me and secretly speculating as to whether I was a good mother. I worried that if I went back to work when my children were young, people would think I was abandoning them. But I also worried that if I didn't go back to work, people would think I was not providing for them. There was no way I could win that one.

In reality, most people do not think or judge us nearly as much as we believe they do. And yet, we spend time worrying about what other people think, rather than worrying about ourselves, or our families. This is just crazy and until you are able to let go of this sense of societal pressure, you may find yourself pulled in so many directions, you end up falling to pieces.

I suggest that you take some time to recognize what expectations may be limiting you and take steps to reverse these effects. It may be that you need to volunteer less time at your child's school or that you have to stop coaching every team sport in your local area. It may be that you just have to stop worrying about what everyone else is thinking and focus on what you need. It may also mean that you have to take time for yourself, away from both your kids and your job, to do something for yourself. It may be impossible for you to nurture a business if you cannot even take time to nurture yourself.

Let go of the need to have other people do things for you personally

As is true for most college students, money was tight for me. I remember eating a regular diet of macaroni and cheese and chicken pot pies. I could make it through the entire month with a food and entertainment allowance of less than fifty dollars. When I got out of college and started making good money, I naturally wanted to reward myself for all the sacrifice and hard effort. Even though my first job earned me only twenty-five thousand dollars a year annually, it felt like a million dollars as far as I was concerned.

I thought I was rich and quickly started to develop different spending habits. I also realized that I didn't have to do things for myself any more. At first, it was just a few things like getting my car washed at the expensive car wash or getting highlights at the local salon. But after my kids were born and more money started rolling in, it changed to become almost everything. I had a maid coming once a week, along with a guy to mow and take care of the lawn. I had a handy man come to install simple things like light fixtures and door handles. I hired people to teach me how to exercise, how to eat right, even how to install my child's car seat properly.

Not only was I spending a huge amount for these services, but I was also becoming accustomed to doing nothing for myself. I was becoming lazy and this was not a good thing. When I finally realized how much money I was wasting, it was like a slap in the face. I realized that my laziness had cost me more than just the money; it had cost me the feeling of empowerment you get from doing things for yourself. That was the greatest loss of all.

I slowly began to ease back into the world of doing things for myself. The entire process, which I now consider to be complete, took about five years. I had really become lazy, mind you. I now do everything for myself. I mow and tend to my own lawn. I cut and even highlight my own hair. Expensive gym memberships have been replaced with a pair of running shoes. I discovered I can repair most things too, instead of replacing them, which is what I used to do.

If you plan on becoming self-employed, I recommend you first evaluate how many services you are paying for in your personal life. Determine which ones you can do for yourself and make an effort to start doing so. Not only will you save money that can be put towards your business, but you will gain the sense of accomplishment and empowerment that comes with doing things for yourself.

Let go of the need for trendy and expensive possessions

In 2008 the New York Times published an article titled, "You are what you spend". The articles authors, Michael Cox and Richard Alm created a graph which outlined how Americans spend their money. The graph divided Americans into the following three groups:

- **The lowest with an annual household income of $9,974**
- **The middle with an annual household income of $44,933**
- **The highest with an annual income of $149,963**

They looked at how much each of these groups were consuming in various categories such as apparel, housing, transportation, health care and entertainment. They found that the lowest group was spending around $18,153 a year; twice the amount they were earning. Even though the spending for the highest group was larger, $69,863, it was only half of their earnings. The middle group did not do much better than the lowest group; over three fourths of their spending was for household consumption. And it may be no surprise for you to learn that consumption has been spreading the quickest for technology-related expenses such as computers, cell phones and the Internet.

The wealthiest are spending most of their money on education, taxes, charitable contributions and investments, or things that go towards building wealth and not just satisfying urges. Living in America is truly a blessing and we are all fortunate for the abundant choices presented here. But, if you want to become a lean, mean, self-employed machine, you need to learn how to resist some of the temptations that surround you every day. When you are starting your own business, money will be tight and you need to be able to withstand the times when no income is coming in. To get your finances straight, which is something I will talk about more in the next chapter, you need to start by examining your spending habits.

The first step towards financial freedom comes from curtailing spending. This means you may have to do without the iPod or the 60 inch flat screen television. But, it doesn't mean you have to start shopping for clothes that are out of style or even stop eating out every week.

What you may have to do instead is get clever about where you shop and look for better bargains. For example, many high-priced clothing retailers will drastically discount clothing items that have not sold within a few weeks. If you are willing to search through racks or bins of clothes, you can pick up well made clothes at a fantastic price. You can also look for a two for one coupon at some of your favorite restaurants. Many restaurants will typically offer these and other good deals to increase business.

Additionally, you can try the following test: the next time you plan to buy something, ask yourself if it is something you need or just something you want. If it is something you just want, then put it down and tell yourself that you will buy it later. You may find that you don't even want it next week and think of all the money you just saved.

Regardless of whether you are self-employed or just thinking about becoming self-employed, adopting good spending habits now will go a long way towards gaining you financial independence.

Let go of the excuses

I recently watched a fantastic show on Public Television called "Excuses Be Gone". The show was hosted by Dr. Wayne Dyer, who is an author and motivational speaker. Dr. Dyer's latest book, also called

"Excuses Be Gone," explains how to change the self-defeating thinking habits that trap all of us in our current situations. The portion of the show that touched me in particular was when Dr. Dyer brought on stage a young man from New Orleans named Dan Caro.

Dan suffered a traumatic event when he was less than two years old. He was severely burned over most of his body and when the doctors removed the bandages from his hands, they literally fell to the floor. Most people might think that Dan would have no chance for having a good life after such a horrible accident, but those people never met Dan.

Despite having challenges that most of us can only imagine in our worst nightmares, he was able to overcome his severe limitations and become an accomplished drummer. Yes, that's right, he's a drummer. Despite having no hands, Dan Caro persevered and on national television, he performed an excellent drum routine that would have rivaled most professional players.

So, next time you tell yourself you can't do something because you are too tired, or you don't have enough money, or you have some kind of handicap, think of Dan Caro. He never let the excuse of having no hands prevent him from doing what he loved, playing music, and you should never let excuses limit what you are capable of.

In the next section, I will profile a woman who exemplifies many of the traits I have mentioned in this chapter. Her name is Chellie Campbell and I am sure she will be as much an inspiration for you as she has been for me.

Chellie Campbell – Creator of the Financial Stress Reduction workshops and author of *The Wealthy Spirit* and *Zero to Zillionaire*

Chellie Campbell didn't start out her life as a financial expert. Far from it. Chellie started out as a musical comedy actress. To support her acting career, she took on secretarial jobs, which led her to discover that she had a knack for bookkeeping. That led her to start her own business and, eventually, to design a series of popular financial stress reduction workshops. Chellie then wrote two best-selling books based on her workshops, "The Wealthy Spirit", and "Zero to Zillionaire".

Chellie's "secret recipe" for success did not come from a fancy financial degree from Harvard, but from her passion and positive attitude. And don't think it was all just good luck either. Chellie had her share of bad luck; she just never let it defeat her. In the 1990's her business tanked, she lost a home to foreclosure and was sitting on a pile of credit card debt. Instead of feeling sorry for herself and giving up, she turned things around. She went on a strict budget and focused on keeping a positive attitude. As a result, she was able to pay off all her bills and get her finances back in great shape.

It is Chellie's first-hand experience with overwhelming debt that makes her so qualified to speak to others about how to get out from under it. Her first book, "The Wealthy Spirit: Daily Affirmations for Financial Stress Reduction", is a page-a-day journey towards financial independence. It is filled with informative and motivational information designed to get someone out of debt and on the road to success.

> *"The secret to success is to pay attention to what life is showing you, and follow your bliss. Make money, do good, and have fun!"*

Chellie's second book, "Zero to Zillionaire: 8 Foolproof Steps to Financial Peace of Mind", is not about making a zillion dollars. It is about achieving the kind of financial independence that allows someone to work, but also to have fun in their lives. As Chellie says, "If you have a zillion dollars but no friends and work that is profitable but isn't fun, you're not a Zillionaire. If you have great friends and fun work but no money, then you're not a Zillionaire, either. My definition of Zillionaire is someone who has a Zillion dreams of infinite possibility, is taking a zillion actions to make them come true, is making as many zillions of dollars as possible, making a zillion friends, doing a zillion good deeds, taking a zillion naps and a zillion vacations, and having a zillion adventures in a long fun-filled life."

If you want to learn more about Chellie and her terrific workshops, check out her web site at http://www.chellie.com.

Letting Go

This chapter summary card contains a list of all the items mentioned in this chapter. If you think you might have trouble letting go of some of the things in this chapter, I suggest you make a copy of this page and paste it up in a place where you will see it every day.

- ❏ **Let go of the blame**
- ❏ **Let go of the fear of failure**
- ❏ **Let go of people that limit or restrict you**
- ❏ **Let go of other people's expectations of you**
- ❏ **Let go of the need to have other people do things for you personally**
- ❏ **Let go of the need for trendy and expensive possessions**
- ❏ **Let go of the excuses**

Luck is when opportunity knocks,
and you answer.

— Anonymous

Chapter 5:

Where to Start?

HOPEFULLY, BY THIS POINT IN THE BOOK you are getting pretty excited about what might lie ahead for you. Naturally, you may be asking, ok, how do I get started? The good news is that you already have. Simply reading this book and imagining what your life could become, you have made the first big step towards achieving your dreams. Thoughts are very powerful, and when you think extensively about something you want, you will soon begin to see that something start to develop.

Select a business

The process of choosing the kind of business to go into varies from person to person. Some people may simply want to establish a business that is a smaller, more personalized version of what they are doing now. For others, starting a business may be an opportunity to do something entirely new.

If you are uncertain about what kind of business you want to establish, let me make a huge suggestion: **pick something that you are absolutely passionate about**. Passion is a strong emotion and therefore a critical motivator for someone that is self-employed. Remember, you will no longer have the things that motivate you in the corporate world like performance reviews, corporate-sponsored retreats or large bonuses. Well, you could still have those things, but you would be the one hosting the retreats and paying the bonus! Self-employment can be hard, so without a passionate interest in your chosen field, it is more likely that you will lose interest and your business will ultimately fail. If your business involves something that you already love, then you will be more tolerant of the low times and more able to sail right through them. As Annette Pelliccio advised in Chapter 2, "Do what you are completely passionate about. In order to succeed and be truly happy, you must love what you do."

All the people I interviewed for this book are doing something that they love, which in turn makes them happy and successful. Bruce Johnson told me, "One of the coolest things about my life is that I get to spend my days doing something that I very much love to do. I believe doing what you love is an important part of having a happy and fulfilling life. So just from that perspective, I consider myself very lucky to have found my niche at an early age."

In addition to selecting something that you love, you should also try to leverage any existing knowledge or skills that you have. Even if you decide to go into a brand new field, it is likely that you have some existing skill or talent that will help you in your new endeavor. For example, if you are good with people, try doing something that involves working with the public, or if you love to keep things in order, do something that requires good organization skills.

If you already have knowledge specific to a particular industry, try to stay within that industry. For example, if you are a trained nurse, don't try to open a restaurant. Instead, try creating a business that can utilize your existing nursing skills, such as being an independent home health care nurse for the elderly.

And finally, whatever you do, don't fall for any get rich quick schemes. The world is full of them right now. Unfortunately, the worst ones are usually associated with the Internet, since disreputable people can hide behind a legitimate looking web site. If you run across an online ad promising you a great deal of money for very little effort; **DO NOT CLICK THE AD**. I'm serious. It's a scam or it's illegal. Ever heard of the phrase, "There ain't no such thing as a free lunch"? Well, it is true. In fact, it is *so* true that I think the phrase should be printed on the front of every dollar bill in America.

Legitimate businesses are founded on solid work and dedication. If you want to build something that will last, get ready to roll up your sleeves and do some good old fashioned hard work. That is the only way you will be able to create something that withstands recessions, wars, and even just bad days. If you are getting discouraged by all the talk about hard work, go back and read chapter 2, because I promise you the hard work will be worth it.

Do your research online

Once you determine what your business will be, you need to spend time deciding how you will establish it. To do this, you need to do as much research as you can into the market potential, as well as the position of your current business competitors. You need to know exactly what your competitors are offering and how much they are charging for it. This is an especially critical step if you are entering a new market or developing a new skill.

One of the best ways to do research these days is on the Internet. Search engines such as Google (http://www.google.com) allow you to enter a few search keywords and retrieve a seemingly endless stream of information. If you do not consider yourself to be Internet savvy, now is the time to change that. Fortunately, search engines are becoming increasingly easier to use since they now try to guess what you are really searching for. They are also pretty good at returning only the most relevant information.

Of course, the more you use the search engines, the better you will get at using them. As Bruce Johnson advises, "because the effective use of Google is much more art than science, make sure you do whatever you can to get yourself familiar with the techniques that will bring the correct answers onto the front page."

I suggest doing searches involving several different keywords, along with different combinations of keywords. For example, if you want to go into the pet grooming business you will want to enter the words "pet grooming" into a search engine. When you do, Google will not only display the relevant results, but it will also list at the bottom of the page a list of related search phrases, such as "pet grooming tools" or "pet grooming business". By clicking on one of these search phrases, along with the original search, you are sure to obtain a much broader range of information.

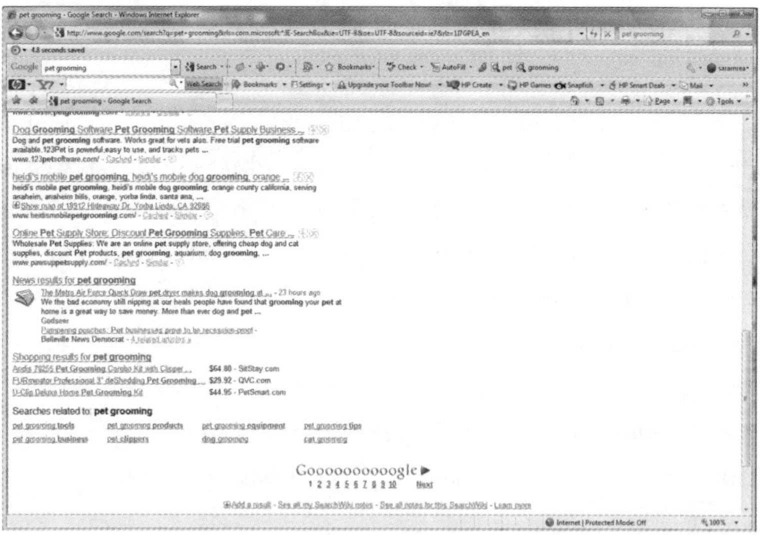

In addition to using related search phrases, I would suggest you check out Google Insights for Search at http://www.google.com/insights/search/#. Google offers some really terrific tools that help you make the most of your browsing experience and Insights for Search is just one of them. The Insights for Search product provides you with some really interesting analytics that can help further your research. For example, it can graphically show you how much interest there has been for your search term over a period of time, as well as what geographic areas have searched for that term the most. This kind of information can be really useful when you are trying to determine the market potential for your business.

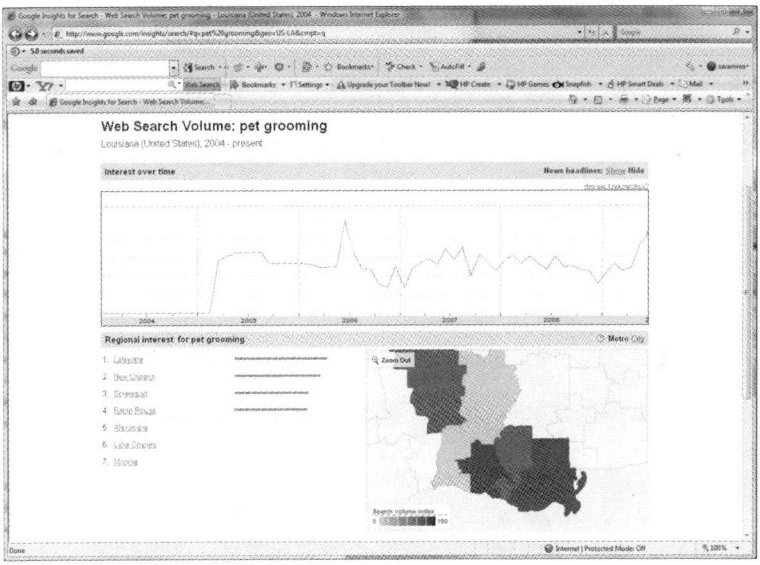

Remember that Google is just one way to search the Internet. New and improved search engines are being developed every day. Each one promises to do a better job at zeroing in on the specific information the user is seeking. The latest search engines are also striving to offer a more natural way of searching by asking questions instead of entering a few keywords.

In June of 2009, Microsoft released a new search engine called Bing (http://www.bing.com). Microsoft claims that Bing is more like a decision engine because it helps the user to make important decisions based on search results. So far, Bing appears to be a decent competitor for Google, but in my opinion does not serve as a replacement. Of course, Microsoft claims there is still more to come with Bing and that eventually it will "Help people make better decisions". Whether that is true remains to be seen.

In the mean time, I would suggest using both Bing and Google when doing your online research. You might also want to watch for other search engines that offer more intuitive ways of searching. The search engine market is a big one and many companies are striving to replace Google as the preferred search engine. Expect to see some big changes and better search products in the weeks and months to come.

Write a business plan

You wouldn't suggest that someone build a house without a plan; the same reasoning applies when building your business. You will need some kind of plan which outlines the nature of your business and how you expect it to grow. The components of this plan depend a lot on what type of business you are selecting and whether you will be seeking any financing or not .

If you are seeking financing through investors or a bank, then your business plan will need to be very formal and precise. People will not be willing to give you any money unless you can prove to them that your business is a sound investment opportunity. Creating a business plan for this purpose is a big process; there are entire books and web sites devoted just to this. There are even people out there you can hire to write your business plan for you. If you know for sure your business will require financing from an outside source, then I suggest you check out some of the following resources:

Small Business Administration – Write a Business Plan

- The following web site, http://www.sba.gov/smallbusinessplanner/plan/writeabusinessplan/index.html will give you detailed information about how to write your business plan and offers an online workshop which tells you how to prepare a business plan.

Business.Gov – Business Loan Checklist

- The Business.gov web site offers an abundance of useful information for business owners. The following link takes you to a checklist of all the things you will need when applying for a loan from a bank, as well as to a link to resources for writing a business plan: http://www.business.gov/finance/financing/loans/loan-checklist.html.

Bplans.com

- This great web site offers a software package called Business Plan Pro (http://www.bplans.com/business_planning_software/), which has over 500 sample business plans that you can use as a template for writing your own business plan. They cover just about every possible industry and, at $99.95 each, are not a bad way to ensure you have all the necessary forms and data in place before applying for your loan.

Even if you will not require financing, you still need some sort of a plan. It does not have to be as formal a plan as the one required for banks, but you do need to sit down and do some heavy thinking before you start this business. At a minimum, you need to ask and answer some of the following questions:

- What products or services will you offer and how much will they cost?
- What level of service do you plan to offer? How can you ensure this level is maintained?
- If you have a product, should you offer a guarantee of some kind and how will you handle refunds or exchanges?
- Who will your customers be and how can you get and keep new customers?
- Where will your business be located and do you always plan for it to be located there?
- What equipment and inventory do you need to establish your business? What do you need to keep it running for a year or two?
- Do you plan to keep it small and just have you as the only employee, or would you like the business to grow and take on numerous employees or consultants?
- If you do intend to hire employees, how many employees do you ultimately want, what will they do and how much will you pay them? Also, how do you think you will locate good employees?
- What kind of roadblocks do you see for starting your business? What about roadblocks that might lie ahead in a year or two? And how will you handle these potential problems?
- How will you handle advertising and marketing of your business? Will this change as your business grows?
- Where would you like for the business to be in one year? Two years, five years?

In addition to answering these questions, you should consider writing a company mission statement. The mission statement should tell clearly what your company does and what it plans to do in the future. It should reflect the company image and tell how your business is different and better than all the others. Not only will writing this statement help you to clarify your thinking, but the statement will make excellent material for your web site or any marketing brochures you may offer.

Consolidate your email addresses

In today's business world, email has almost replaced the telephone as a means of effective business communication. Not only is it a convenient way to communicate, but it also provides a paper trail that can be vital to the small business owner. One missed email can sometimes break a company. That is why it is very important that you have a plan from the beginning to manage multiple email addresses.

Chances are you have established two or more email addresses through free email accounts like Microsoft's Live Mail, Google's Gmail, AOL's AIM Mail or Yahoo mail. You may also have an email account assigned to you through your Internet provider. Additionally, you may be hanging on to an email account from a current or former employer. Logging into all these email accounts and trying to keep straight which one is for personal use and which one is for business use can easily become a nightmare.

Before you start your business and acquire yet one more email address, you should plan to consolidate and manage all those email addresses. I suggest establishing one email address to act as your central address. This will be an email address you will keep for a long time. Emails from all other accounts can then be forwarded to this email address.

You can then manage all the emails from one single account, which can contain multiple folders to store and organize all those emails.

I would suggest that you not use one of the free services for this central account and instead pay for a permanent account that includes considerable storage space. This eliminates the possibility of your free account being discontinued, and reduces the likelihood that you will have only a limited amount of storage space available to you. Some of the free accounts out there do offer unlimited storage space, but I question whether that will always be the case if you are not paying for the account.

I personally use a paid account from Microsoft's Live Mail that extends to me as much storage space as I need. I have emails saved from 5 years ago in some of my folders. I access this account through a web browser, but I could use desktop client software such as Microsoft Outlook if I preferred. I like using the browser, since I use multiple machines and am frequently working remotely; I do not want the hassle of realizing an email I downloaded to my machine at home is not available to me while I am elsewhere.

The email service you select and how you view the emails is not as important as having one central account that you will keep for a very long time. This will not only help you avoid missing any crucial emails, but it will also save you the stress of having to notify all your contacts every time your email address changes. It will also give you a central place to store all your contacts, which can be very beneficial when there is a need to make some big announcement about your new business.

Establish a web presence

As a web developer, it is obvious that the Internet is a central part of my life; it is for many other people in the world as well. Some customers will not even consider doing business with a web site-less company. Even if your business is not technology-based and has nothing to do with the Internet, you still need to have a web site. It is almost equivalent to a business card these days.

The web site you build does not have to be fancy with all sorts of flash-based graphics or large databases, but it does have to be professional and neat looking. It also should reflect current trends in web site design and not as if it was designed in the 1990's. It should include key information about your business, such as the following:

- **Contact Information** - Include phone numbers, physical addresses and email addresses

- **About the Company** – Tell about yourself and include a resume or give a company history

- **Product or Service Information** – Tell about what you are selling and how much it costs. You do not have to sell your services or product online, but you do need to tell the customer how they can obtain what you offer.

The web site should also be easy to navigate and intuitive to use. No one should have to search for your service and product information. Most people adopt the 3-click rule, which means no information should be more than 3-clicks away from the home page.

Now, I realize that I told you to be cautious about major expenses, but trust me; this is one expense you do not want to be too frugal about. Do not make the common mistake that many small business owners do and allow a friend to design your web site. This is a task best handled by a professional, who should be able to do an excellent job in a timely manner.

Unless you are a web developer or web designer yourself, you should consider hiring a company or an individual consultant specializing in web site design. There are many companies and consultants capable of building a custom or template-based web site, but as with every business, the buyer should beware. It would be wise to use a company with referrals and recommendations from satisfied clients; check to see that they are helpful for the small business owner. I ran across this web design consultant that I would recommend to small business owners: Aldebaran Website Design (http://aldebaranwebdesign.com/).

Run by Jill Olkoski, Aldebaran Website Design has a sound approach and, most importantly, she specializes in development for the small business owner. She can help you build a new web site or renovate an old one that may have been badly designed or is simply outdated. She can also help you with Search Engine Optimization (SEO), which means you are placed higher on the results page for a search engine such as Google. SEO is one of the most important aspects of web design, and is all too often overlooked.

However, use caution before you go out and pay any one a lot of money for SEO services. There are many sharks in Internet waters, and many disreputable people and companies that may take advantage of you. Before investing in any SEO service, read this Search Engine Optimization Starter Guide document:

(http://www.google.com/webmasters/docs/search-engine-optimization-starter-guide.pdf). This document may enable you to do what is necessary without paying an SEO service an expensive monthly fee.

If you look for another company or consultant to create and maintain your web site, it is best to look for a "web designer" or "graphics designer." "Web developers" typically are back-end developers, meaning they do a lot of the work behind the scenes with databases and heavy code. Web designers tend to be more graphics oriented people, who focus more on aesthetics and less on functionality. If your website is serving primarily as a way to present yourself to the world, then a designer is your best choice. If your website will need more functionality, such as the ability to sell goods online and track customers, then you may need both a web developer and a web designer.

Web designers are optimal for small businesses for two reasons. First, web designers tend to be less expensive; if you are just starting your business and revenues are still modest, this is an important consideration for you. Secondly, web developers tend to be not as proficient at design work; instead, they focus their programming skills on over-complicating things (bless our hearts) creating solutions that just might be overkill. Just being honest here!

If you are still considering designing the web site yourself or having a friend do it for you, then I suggest you check out the Office Live Small Business Community web site. They have a section with some informative and well-written how-to-articles (http://ask.officelive.com/smallbusiness/wiki/articles/default.aspx) that should help guide you in the right direction.

Joan Roberts: Certified Career Management Coach and Owner of CareerCounseling.com

Joan Roberts is one lucky lady. In 1992, she quit her job to pursue an entrepreneurial dream of owning her own career consulting business. At first, she worked with other consultants to provide outplacement services to large businesses, but then in 1995 she got her big break. She managed to snag the domain name CareerCounseling.com and since then her business has shifted to operate primarily online. Owning the CareerCounseling domain name means that when someone types in "career counseling" into a search engine, Joan's web site comes up first.

In the online search world, being on the first search page, let alone the first position of the first search page, can make the difference between success and failure. For Joan, it has meant she now has the opportunity to do what she loves, helping other people realize their dreams, while also providing for her family and being able to devote a lot of her time to them.

Of course Joan does not just sit back and let the Internet do all the work. She considers word-of-mouth referrals to be the biggest source of her business. As she said, "Nothing speaks volumes like a happy customer with lots of friends."

Joan mostly works with clients to determine where they want to go in their careers. To do this, she performs career testing and relies specifically on the Myers-Briggs Type indicator to help examine a person's strengths and weaknesses. Often she is approached by clients wanting to become self-employed. She advises these clients to approach self-employment slowly and to try and get their business up and running while still employed. As she puts it, "That makes for a much easier transition financially, although it's a tough few months with burning the candle on both ends. However, the payoff is typically worth it."

> *"Self-employment income is more like a roller-*
> *coaster ride, some highs and some lows,*
> *but it all balances out at the end of the year."*

It certainly has been worth it for Joan. She told me that she loves being a self-employed career coach and says, "I am successful and feel terrific every day about helping people propel themselves forward in their careers." For more information about Joan and her services visit http://www.careercounseling.com.

Where to Start

This chapter summary card contains a list of all the items mentioned in this chapter. I suggest you make a copy of this page and paste it up in a place where you will see it every day.

- ❑ **Select a business**
- ❑ **Do your research online**
- ❑ **Write a business plan**
- ❑ **Consolidate your email addresses**
- ❑ **Establish a web presence**

A ship is safe in harbor,
but that's not what ships are for.

–William Shedd

Chapter 6:

Good Advice

In this chapter I will share some good advice for self-employed people that I have encountered while researching this book. In some cases, the recommendations are simple things to remember, such as trust your instincts; in other cases, they involve specific things you should do, such as get your finances straight.

Trust your instincts

In January of 2007, the University College of London (UCL) issued a press release regarding research that was published in the journal *Current Biology*. The results of the research showed clearly that people have a definite advantage when they use their instincts to make decisions versus rational thought. In the study participants were asked to identify symbols presented to them. When they were given no time to make a decision, the results were more accurate than when they were given plenty of time to make their decisions.

This may seem strange to you, but as Dr. Li Zhaoping of the UCL Department of Psychology states, "You would expect people to make more accurate decisions when given the time to look properly. Instead they performed better when given almost no time to think. The conscious or top-level function of the brain, when active, vetoes our initial subconscious decision – even when it is correct – leaving us unaware or distrustful of our instincts and at an immediate disadvantage. Falling back on our inbuilt, involuntary subconscious processes for certain tasks is actually more effective than using our higher-level cognitive functions."

This is good news for the self-employed, since we often have little time to make decisions. Instead of slowing down your progress by questioning every decision you make, choose to feel confident that the instinctual decisions you are making are probably the best ones.

Become a feedback machine

For some people, accepting criticism is impossible. They would rather be dead wrong than be criticized for any fault. For most of us, the ability to accept criticism is a skill we develop as we mature. For writers like me, it is critical to develop that skill early on, since incorporation of criticism is fundamental to good writing.

In order to thrive in your business, you too must be willing to accept and incorporate feedback early on. The feedback will likely come from your customers, but you may also seek feedback from others. Each time someone offers you input or advice, you need to be ready to listen to that feedback and then determine whether it represents a change you need to make.

You will need to actively seek feedback by regularly asking your customers how their experience was. You can ask for feedback through a customer experience form, or you can just informally ask your customers if they are happy with your service or product. Also, do not limit feedback opportunities to customers alone. Ask for feedback from suppliers or work associates.

The only way you can improve yourself and what you have to offer is to identify what your weaknesses are. We all have weaknesses, so do not think you are uniquely able to do everything right. There is always room for improvement. Do not be afraid to identify what your weaknesses are. Doing so will not make you weak, but rather will give you the opportunity to become stronger than ever.

If it helps, think of yourself as a feedback machine; constantly taking in input from the world around you, processing that input, and then in some cases performing an action as a result. Do not think of the input as negative or a criticism against you personally. Just accept that the input may or may not be valuable to you and try to separate yourself from the emotional aspect of it.

Don't be afraid to do something that has no immediate financial payback

When I decided to write my first book, I had no idea what to expect. I was in no way prepared for the amount of time it would take. And, I was certainly not prepared for the fact that I would end up earning less than $5000 when all was said and done. Considering that it took me over one year to write and, in my estimation, around 600 hours of effort, that amounts to an hourly rate of $8.33.

Despite the fact that writing that first book was not financially beneficial, the experience certainly benefited me tremendously. Writing that first book established my name and gave me credibility that would have taken many more years to develop as a consultant alone. It also opened doors and gave me the courage to explore opportunities I might not have attempted otherwise.

Like me, Mark Dunn had to do things that provided no immediate payback. As he said, "I spent about three years in lower paying jobs while I was building real world skills on my resume. I worked really long hours during that time and was constantly trying to pick up new techniques and learn anything I could from other programmers around me."

It is very common for someone starting a business to make initial monetary sacrifices in an effort to build more business. For this reason, some people find it easier to start pursuing their new business while already employed full time. It can mean extra work and really long hours for a while, but in the end it can result in a payback that lasts a lifetime.

Accept help from others

As Joan Roberts, the Certified Career Management Coach I introduced in Chapter 3 indicated, self-employed people are typically go-getters. This type of person tends to be very competent at what they do and therefore they may be tempted to accept too much responsibility in the initial days of starting their business. For some people, this can be a costly mistake.

It may be necessary for you to accept help from other people when you are first starting your business, and even after it has been established for a while. Annette Pelliccio offers this advice, "Don't try to perfect your weaknesses – hire people who have strengths where you are lacking. Don't try to do it all! It just doesn't work."

If you have family and friends offering to help with your business, take them up on the offer. Even if there are no opportunities for them to help with your business, they may be able to help you in your personal life as you get settled into your new role. Don't let pride stand in your way.

Adopt a healthy lifestyle

As I will discuss further in Chapter 7, self-employed people should expect higher premiums for their health insurance. For most people this means accepting a high deductible insurance plan. As a mother of three young children, this was an obvious concern for me when I first made the jump to self-employment.

I am fortunate in that my children and I are naturally healthy and none of us has suffered from any chronic health problems. However, I firmly believe that you cannot take your good health for granted. For several years I have made vigilant efforts towards promoting a healthy lifestyle for myself and my children. This means encouraging regular exercise and ensuring that we all eat properly. As a result, doctor visits for my family are typically only preventative in nature.

Medical costs are skyrocketing and this is a huge problem for our society. At the same time, many people suffer from obesity and stress related health problems. If you are considering a jump to self-employment and you are not in the best of health, you may want to consider adopting a healthy lifestyle as one of your top priorities. Not only will you maintain better physical health, but your mental health should improve as well, thus strengthening your resolve and ability to achieve success.

Roger Arrick advises, "Seek balance and a lifestyle that can be sustained instead of the race-n-crash method honored by so many these days". Roger suggests that self-employed people consider getting at least eight hours of sleep at night one of their work responsibilities. This will help to ensure you are fully prepared and in top creative form.

Roger also suggests that self-employed people consume a healthy diet that consists of lots of whole, natural foods, while also avoiding processed food and stimulants. As Roger states, "our bodies are biological machines, so feed them the food they are designed for. Filling a car with aviation fuel may result in great performance for a little while, but soon the valves will need replacing. Our human bodies do not need a stimulant to perform and create."

I am a busy person and I do not have a lot of time to prepare extravagant meals. The good news is that you do not have to eat badly just because you don't have a lot of extra time. One of my favorite things to eat for lunch is a spinach and mushroom wrap that takes less than two minutes to prepare. It tastes delicious and provides all the healthy nutrients my brain and body need.

The spinach and mushroom wrap is dead simple to make. Just take a plain tortilla and use a spoon to spread one tablespoon of olive oil all over the surface. Next, take a handful of fresh spinach, which you can get from Wal-Mart already washed and prepared. Add the spinach to the tortilla, along with a few mushrooms and a handful of two percent shredded cheese. If you prefer meat with your wrap, you can also add a slice of turkey or chicken. Finish it off with a little of your favorite spice and place in the microwave for one minute. When it is done, just wrap it up and you have a quick and healthy meal, which you can also enjoy with some baked potato chips.

Surround yourself with things that inspire you

Considering the recent recession, everyone is in need of a little inspiration these days. This can be especially true for the newly self-employed or for those business owners struggling through a down time in the market. As I discussed in Chapter 3, it is essential that the self-employed person think like an optimist. This may not always be an easy thing to do and so it helps if you surround yourself with things that inspire and encourage you.

Have you ever noticed that when you buy a new car, you suddenly start seeing that same make and model everywhere you go? The same kind of thing happens when you start looking for things that inspire you. The world is full of happy and positive people and good things happen every day. If you actively seek out these people and things, you may start to see the world in an entirely new light.

If you happen to live in a very negative and depressed place, it may take some extra effort on your part to seek out inspiration. If this is the case, you can start simply by posting an inspirational message somewhere you will see it every day, such as on your refrigerator or in your car. I have included some inspirational quotes at the start of each chapter, but here are a few more of my favorites that you might want to consider writing down and posting somewhere you can see them.

> *"Action may not always bring happiness,*
> *but there is no happiness without action."*
>
> — Benjamin Disraeli

> *"Failure is only the opportunity to begin again,*
> *this time more wisely."*
>
> —Anonymous

> *"The highest reward for man's toil is not*
> *what he gets for it, but what he becomes by it."*
>
> —John Ruskin

> *"If your ship doesn't come in, swim out to it."*
>
> —Jonathan Winters

> *"Courage is going from failure to failure*
> *without losing enthusiasm."*
>
> —Winston Churchill

> *"If you only look at what is, you might never*
> *attain what could be."*
>
> —Anonymous

"Always bear in mind that your own resolution to succeed is more important than any one thing."

—Abraham Lincoln

You can also start listening to inspirational music. I happen to find Will Smith's song, "It's all good" particularly inspiring. Whenever I am having a bad day or starting to doubt myself, I play that song and it always makes me feel better. I also find Jason Mraz's music very inspiring. I am particularly fond of a song titled, "Live High". Look for songs that inspire you and make sure you have them available when you need a quick boost.

Schedule breaks and stick to them

Alex Cook advises people considering self-employment to "learn time-management or time will manage you." He told me, "The worst part of working for yourself is that any time you are not working, you feel like you should be working. It gives what you do a certain pioneer zeal that I never had at full-time jobs, but it can also burn you out quickly."

I too have noticed the pressure to always be doing or producing something. In some ways this pressure can be good, since it keeps you moving forward, but if not handled properly, it can have negative effects. It can be very easy for self-employed people working at home to get carried away and find themselves working all day and night.

To prevent this from happening to you, I would suggest making an effort to set aside a specific time of the day when you will absolutely NOT do anything work related. Exactly how much time is up to you, but I would suggest a minimum of one hour a day. The time can be broken out into several breaks or taken all at once.

If you are a parent, make sure that you do not ignore yourself during these times and just tend to the house or the kids. Burning yourself out will not do anyone any favors. It will just make you cranky and hard to deal with. This will likely make you prone to errors and the result could be very bad for your business and for your family.

Setting aside time for yourself will not only help you to manage stress, but it can be a great time for coming up with creative ideas for your business. Don't dedicate the time to thinking of ideas, but be aware that they may just occur to you spontaneously when you are taking time for yourself. I suggest getting out once a day for a walk in the fresh air. Turn off the cell phone and make an effort to take these walks even when the workload is high. You are your business's greatest asset and it is fundamental that you be in top working order.

Decrease your debt substantially

According to the United States Census Bureau, there were 159 million credit card holders in the United States in the year 2000. Six years later that number jumped to 173 million and the US Census Bureau expects the number will reach 181 million by the year 2010. This is remarkable growth.

Although the growth part is good in some ways, it can also be bad when Americans are consistently spending more than they earn. The result is too much debt that will be almost impossible to pay back. The current economic recession indicates how serious the consequences of spending too much, too fast can be. Each of us has a personal responsibility to decrease our own debt substantially.

The problem with debt is more than just the very high finance fees. People suffering from too much debt also have limited options when it comes to financing their businesses. High debt and late payments can quickly result in lowered credit scores, which can prevent people from getting necessary small business loans. Too much debt also creates stress that can have disastrous effects on your health and overall self-confidence.

I recommend that everyone, whether they think they have a problem with debt or not, sit down and do a thorough debt evaluation. If you have multiple credit cards, try to find ways to consolidate them. In reality you should only have two credit cards; one for personal use, and another for your business. All the others should be paid off or consolidated.

You should also try to get to the point where you are paying off the credit card every month and avoiding finance fees all together. You will never be able to get ahead in your business if you are stuck paying multiple credit cards with high interest rates. Do whatever you can now to reduce or eliminate your debt entirely.

In this next section I will introduce you to a truly free thinker named Alex Cook. Alex clearly demonstrates how doing your own thing can be very rewarding.

Alex Cook – Independent Software Developer, freelance music writer and author of *Darkness Racket* and *Twang*

I first met Alex Cook when I was working for a financial company that eventually went bankrupt. Since then, we have worked together at other companies and I cannot think of another developer that I would recommend more. Alex is the type of person that stands out from all the rest. He is very smart, but also highly creative and talented in both art and music. In fact, it is his original art work that is featured on the front cover of my first book.

Alex holds a bachelor of science in Computer Science, but he also minored in both philosophy and English Literature. For many years Alex worked as a software developer, building up his skill set; for a short time he worked for Microsoft. It wasn't until he was laid off by two companies (Microsoft not being one of them) that he started working as a full-time contractor. At the same time, he pursued his passion for music as a freelance music journalist. In 2006 his first book "Darkness, Racket and Twang" was published, which includes some of his best musical critiques.

As Alex puts it, "I jumped into self-employment contracting out of necessity and did it for three years. It made me realize that anything I want to do in life is up to me. I cannot wait around for promotions or the projects I want, I have to make those happen. "

> *"I think a willingness to tackle something you don't initially understand is the biggest asset you can have in a career."*

Alex was the person that first turned me on to the idea of living with fewer material possessions. It seems that material possessions have a way of owning you more than you own them. Owning a lot of things, especially expensive things, may lock you into a certain lifestyle that for some is unsustainable, which prevents them from pursuing their dreams. Alex taught me that living with less means living more.

Alex recently returned to the world of full-time employment, but this time on his own terms. "I recently started working full-time for a university, but that came out of my presenting them with an idea of what I wanted to do for them rather than just taking a job posted on a website, and that has worked out for me rather well. I came to realize that successful people do not work for a company, they make a company work for them", says Alex.

Good Advice

This chapter summary card contains a list of all the items mentioned in this chapter. I suggest you make a copy of this page and paste it up in a place where you will see it every day.

- ❑ **Trust your instincts**
- ❑ **Become a feedback machine**
- ❑ **Don't be afraid to do something that has no immediate financial payback**
- ❑ **Accept help from others**
- ❑ **Adopt a healthy lifestyle**
- ❑ **Surround yourself with things that inspire you**
- ❑ **Schedule breaks and stick to them**
- ❑ **Decrease your debt substantially**

If there is no struggle,
there is no progress.

—Frederick Douglass

Chapter 7:

Things to Consider

UP TO THIS POINT, we have focused on general preparation tasks which you must do to successfully go into business. In this chapter, we will go into detail about specific expenses you must consider, such as start-up costs, taxes, and insurance. As you read this chapter, keep in mind that the more cost-effective your business is, the lower your prices will be for your customers. If your prices are lower than your competitors' prices, you can compete with them even if you cannot match their potentially big marketing and advertising budgets. Small businesses are more likely to succeed when they work smarter, not necessarily harder.

It is possible for you to compete successfully with larger firms if you constantly look for ways to streamline your business and minimize expenses. Approach all major expenditures with caution and always look for ways to postpone taking on major costs, such as hiring new employees, renting or buying office space, and creating large inventories.

Start-up Costs

The total cost of starting a small business will vary quite a bit among different business types and different industries. The expense depends on very basic decisions, such as whether you will operate as a sole proprietor and work from your home, or if you plan to hire employees and rent an office space.

I was fortunate because the start-up costs required for a software consultant are typically very small. Since I had written several articles and one book before making the jump to being a full-time consultant, I had already established a pretty complete home office equipped with a computer, internet connection, and fax machine. This reduced my start-up costs considerably.

Not everyone will be this lucky and therefore start-up costs may be a major concern as you consider self-employment. Many small businesses fail because their owners miscalculate the amount of capital required to start and sustain the business until it begins to realize a profit. Therefore, a first step for anyone considering self-employment is a thorough evaluation of what their start-up costs might be. The best way to do this is to talk to other people in your geographic region who have started businesses in the same industry. You do not have to restrict yourself to people who have been successful in their businesses. In fact, talking with people who have failed can offer valuable insight into common mistakes to avoid. I therefore recommend locating people, who are (or have been) in a similar business, operating in an area with roughly equivalent costs of living.

When calculating your costs, make sure to include initial costs as well as any expenditure necessary to operate your business for the first six to twelve months, as it is prudent to assume that it will take some time to make a profit. For example, if you are renting office space, you will have to include rent and utility costs for at least six months in your start-up costs.

I will discuss some of your start-up costs in greater detail in the remainder of this chapter, but the following list will give you a rough idea of what to consider:

- **Taxes**
- **Insurance**
- **Licenses**
- **Incorporation costs**
- **Accounting**
- **Office equipment**
- **Rent and Utilities**
- **Marketing and Promotional costs**
- **Initial Inventory if you are dealing with a product**

For more information about what start-up costs you need to consider, refer to the following online resources:

Small Business Administration Small Business Planner

- This helpful site includes a link to an online start-up cost calculator. The site also contains useful information about how to plan your business and write a business plan. Refer to the following link: http://www.sba.gov/smallbusinessplanner/start/financestartup/index.html

Microsoft Small Business Center

- Microsoft sponsors a terrific web site dedicated to the small business owner. The site offers valuable advice as well as great offers on software. Check it out at http://www.microsoft.com/smallbusiness/hub.mspx.

New York Times Small Business Resource Center

- A place where small business owners can get valuable information on things like health care, financing, marketing, and even e-commerce. Be sure to check out the newest addition to this site, a web blog called, "You're the Boss". You can get to the web site through the following link: http://www.nytimes.com/pages/business/smallbusiness/index.html

Forming a Corporation

One of the first things you will need to decide when starting your own business is whether or not you will incorporate. Doing so means you have to decide what type of organization you will form; you may want to hire an attorney to help you select a name and file the correct paperwork. Although you do not have to incorporate right away, there are many advantages to doing so that you may want to consider. The biggest reason is that incorporating your business is the best way to legally separate your personal life from your business; this protects you from damaging lawsuits that could be financially catastrophic.

The type of organization you form depends on several things. The following is a list of federally recognized designations and some general reasons for choosing one type over another:

Sole Proprietorship

- This is the simplest type of business to set up and operate. It is typically the choice of independent consultants, freelancers, and individually owned small businesses. The business and the proprietor are legally one entity and the owner has full liability for the company's debts. A way to avoid this is to become a Limited Liability Company (LLC), in which the owner is legally separate from the company and cannot be held responsible for the company's debts. Forming an LLC means you are an unincorporated business and that you will file your income and expenses on a Form 1040 Schedule C when filing your federal taxes. In this case the income is passed on to the proprietor, avoiding the tax consequences of forming a corporation.

Partnerships

- Like sole proprietorships, partnerships are unincorporated and are also considered a Limited Liability Company (LLC). A partnership will have at least two shareholders and each assumes liability for the business in proportion to their percentage ownership. This kind of organization distributes its profits differently than corporations, so you need to check with someone knowledgeable about applicable laws before making the decision whether to form a partnership or a corporation.

S-Corporations

- Similar to a partnership, the S-corporation must have at least one shareholder, but no more than 100. Forming an S-Corporation may have advantages over an LLC for the purposes of paying reduced self-employment taxes. Before selecting this type of organization, I would suggest meeting with a knowledgeable and trusted taxation expert.

Corporations

- These are for-profit, incorporated businesses in which the company has full discretion over the amount of profit they distribute or retain. These businesses must have at least one shareholder. Business owners will likely choose this option when they plan to take a company public or if they need to raise money from investors. A corporation may also be more attractive when there is a desire to provide stock options to key employees

The biggest downside to this type of organization is that the income is subject to double taxation, as the net income of the company is subject to taxes, as well as the money distributed to owners as personal income and dividends

Trusts

- These are usually formed after someone dies and they can be used to designate a portion of funds towards some investment or business activity.

Non-Profits

- As the name suggests this type of organization exists for the public good; they can range from non-profit hospitals to charitable foundations. Non-profit companies are exempt from federal and state taxation, and are required to do substantial documentation and reporting of their activities, income and assets to ensure that they are functioning as a legitimate charity.

Whatever business model you choose, whether or not you hire an attorney depends greatly on how comfortable you are with filing the paperwork yourself. You can create your company without an attorney and many people do so, but I opted to hire a local attorney who ensured that the name I had chosen was not already in use. He also put together all the necessary paperwork; all I had to do was sign a few documents. It was easy and only cost me $500. However, in my research for this book, I discovered that some attorneys charge a lot more than $500 for something you could potentially do yourself with some research.

Another option is to use one of the many online services now available. Many of them allow you to setup an LLC for less than $100, or in some cases for no fee. I would caution you to first make sure the business is legitimate before giving them any money. You can do this by checking for simple things such as contact information or a physical address. If the business lists neither of these, that should be a big red flag for you. Also, take the time to look up the owner of the domain name by going to www.whois.com and typing in the name of the domain. Once you get the Who Is information, do a quick

Google search to see if the person listed on the domain registration has any pending lawsuits or is called out on someone's blog as being a scam artist. A little common sense can go a long way in determining whether a web-based business is legitimate.

If you are interested in filing the paperwork yourself, then I suggest you start by visiting your state's tax agency web site, as you will need to know the laws for your particular state. Keep in mind that the reasons I listed above for choosing one organization over another are not exhaustive. There are entire books and web sites devoted to selecting what your organization should be. Before committing to anything, do your research and check with other people who have done this type of thing before.

Taxes

According to the Internal Revenue Service web site, "Self-employment tax (SE tax) is a social security and Medicare tax primarily for individuals who work for themselves. It is similar to the social security and Medicare taxes withheld from the pay of most wage earners." The current tax rate is 15.3%, of which 12.4 % goes towards social security and 2.9% goes towards Medicare.

Self-employment tax is probably the most surprising thing to people new to self-employment. Roger Arrick told me, "One of the biggest problems for me early on was preparing for quarterly tax payments. It can be painful to make a tax payment when you really need to buy more inventory or need to add another employee."

As Roger mentions, the angst associated with quarterly tax payments can be great, but they are the optimal choice when you are self-employed. Not only do they help you avoid penalties that can be assessed when you file your taxes at the end of the year, but they also distribute the tax burden among four payments, rather than having it due in one lump sum. Quarterly tax payments are essentially estimated taxes, in which the self-employed person must predict what they will earn for the coming year and then divide that amount among four payments.

Before you can pay quarterly tax payments, you must have a social security number (SSN) or an employer identification number (EIN). Most everyone born these days is assigned a social security number at birth, something done when the hospital provides parents the forms to file, but only those people who apply specifically for a EIN will have one. The EIN is used to identify businesses and you will apply for this when you file the paperwork to incorporate your business.

Anyone operating a trade or business, or is operating as an independent contractor, part-time or full-time, is considered self-employed. Essentially if you are working for someone who is paying you money and the employer is not withholding taxes for you, then you must pay the taxes yourself.

To figure out what amount to pay, you need to estimate what your expected adjusted gross income will be. You will also need to determine how much of that income is taxable by looking at what credits and deductions are available to you. If this is your first time doing these calculations, I would suggest that you make an appointment with a local Certified Public Accountant (CPA). Bring them any information you have about how much you expect to earn in the next year. For a small fee, typically around $200, they can help you determine how much your quarterly taxes will be and they may even provide you with the forms you need to send the payments.

If you use a tax program such as H & R Block's Tax Cut, the program can generate your quarterly tax payment forms. This is a real convenience once you have an idea of what your tax payments are likely to be. You simply plug in the estimated quarterly amount and the program produces the forms all ready to be mailed.

The last important thing to remember is that taxes should not be something you put off until the end of the year. As Bruce Johnson says, "Unlike the vast majority of the population, you will not have a steady paycheck. Income will arrive in fits and starts. You need to be diligent in your financial planning to make sure that you don't come up short for your monthly bills or at the end of the year when your taxes are due."

To find out more information about what the Internal Revenue Service expects from you, visit their Small Business and Self-Employed Tax Center web site at http://www.irs.gov/businesses/small/index.html.

Accounting and Invoices

One of the most important aspects of your business involves collecting the money that is owed to you. Because it is so important, you want to make sure you are set up properly from the very beginning. Before you accept the first payment for your product or services, you need to get yourself some sort of an accounting system. It is unnecessary to hire a big accounting firm, but you will likely have to pay for some sort of computer software that helps you manage your customers, invoices, vendors and expenses.

Many small businesses underestimate the importance of a good accounting system. They may attempt to track expenses and invoices using a manual system such as a pen and paper or even a homemade spreadsheet. In many cases the small business owner will quickly become overwhelmed, and they lose track of to whom they owe money and who owes them money—both mistakes that may cost them their business. To avoid this problem while continuing to minimize expenses, I suggest that small businesses consider getting an online subscription to Intuit's QuickBooks.

QuickBooks (http://quickbooks.intuit.com/) is without a doubt the best financial software package on the market today. Several different products are offered, tailored for the small business owner. They even offer a free version of their Simple Start product, which you can access through the following URL: http://quickbooks.intuit.com/product/accounting-software/free-accounting-software.jsp.

I personally use the QuickBooks Online Basic subscription, which you can try for free by using the following URL: http://oe.quickbooks.com/bookkeeping-accounting-systems/?sc=QBC-V51-TRY-FAM-TXT-PROA-081219. Since it is online, that means all you need to manage your finances is a web browser and an Internet connection. The basic software package, which at this writing costs only $9.95/month, allows you to create invoices and manage customer payments and expenses. You can also use the software to manage an unlimited number of customers and vendors. (Note that the free version only

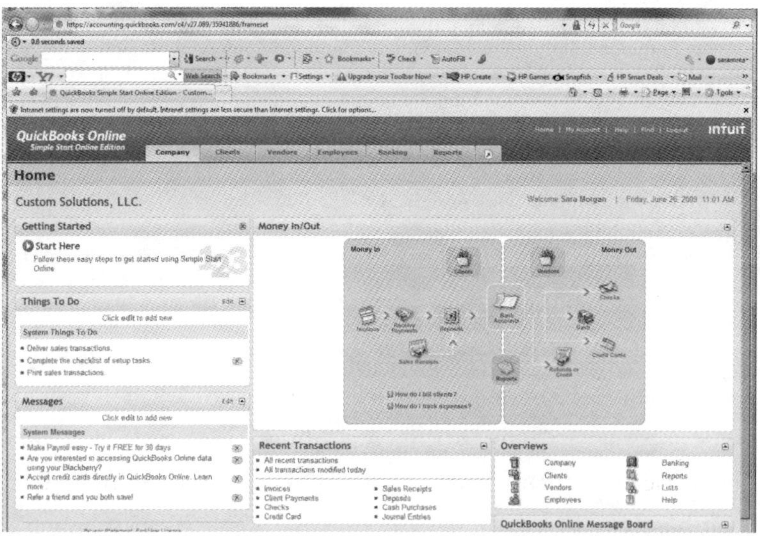

allows you to manage up to 20 customers.) The basic package also offers you 40 standard reports that will help you determine everything from your profitability and the value of your business to detailing what transactions were completed for each customer.

In addition to getting the right software, you need to get the right attitude. Accounts Receivable is going to become a big part of your business. Let's face it, your business is there to make money and if you do not pay enough attention to the payment collection aspect of your business, you may soon be out of business.

As Mark Dunn told me, "I learned some hard lessons early on regarding collections. We had one customer that ran up a bill with nine training classes and then declared bankruptcy without paying. I became very careful about my accounts receivable after that. I also look into the health of companies that are more than 30 days out and want new work. I've also had some trouble with subcontractors not delivering and straining customer relationships. As a result, I'm very careful about monitoring subcontractor work and looking deep into their backgrounds before having them do work under my name. "

When starting a new business it is very easy to focus your efforts solely on what you are providing, yet there are many other aspects of your business that require your attention as well. If you take time early on to evaluate how you will handle your finances, you may save yourself a lot of heartache in the end.

Business Insurance

Depending on the type of business you have, you may need to purchase additional insurance to cover your new venture. It is common for businesses to purchase general liability insurance if they are open to the public or have employees. This type of insurance can protect the company from litigation resulting from accidents or injuries that occur on the business property, as well as damage resulting from exposure to the company's products.

Roger Arrick knows all too well how vulnerable you can become as a business owner. He told me, "Once, one of my employees had a car accident driving their own personal vehicle on a personal trip and I was included in the lawsuit. I survived that thanks to State Farm (I owe them a plug!), but I would have probably shut the company down and become a farmer if this ever happened to me without insurance."

Even if you are an individual contractor, operating without publicly accessible property and with no employees you may still need some form of business insurance. If your client is a large company, they may insist that you show proof of insurance before you can do work for them. Some may require general liability insurance and others may require professional liability insurance.

Professional Liability insurance can protect you from being sued for anything that happens while you are rendering your services. Typically this is used to protect professionals from lawsuits involving breach of contract or negligence. The thing that is important to remember is that even if you are in the right, the cost of hiring an attorney to defend yourself against a lawsuit can be very expensive.

Many insurance companies offer a variety of business insurance policies. Which one you need, if any, depends on the type of business you have and the degree of your risk exposure. For example, you may need commercial auto insurance if you or your employees need to operate a vehicle while conducting business. You might also need workers' compensation insurance if you or your employees perform activities that could result in injury, such as those performed by electricians or manual laborers.

Additionally, each state has their own laws regarding what types of insurance your business may be required to maintain, so check with your State's government web site before making any final decisions. As with any major expense, first consider whether you really need a particular insurance policy before getting one. If you decide one is necessary, make sure you read all the fine print before signing a contract with any insurance agent. Do not assume the policy will cover you in the case of all lawsuits. Some policies are written with as many exclusions as there are inclusions.

Health Insurance

Many people accept that we as a nation are facing a health care crisis. Even if Congress achieves health care reform, the effects of those reforms will likely not be felt for some time. In the meantime, businesses are facing ever-increasing insurance premiums as the cost for health care continues to rise.

If you are unemployed or self-employed, the premiums for health care are even higher. This fact alone can cause some people to forgo any self-employment dreams. While I sympathize with people's concerns, I do not believe anyone should dismiss their dreams just because the cost of insurance will be higher. While it is true that you will have to pay high premiums in order to secure health insurance equal to what you had as a full time employee, you can always opt for a health plan with fewer benefits.

I used to say that said I could never do without a premium health insurance package, and although that was somewhat true while I was pregnant, it is certainly not true now. For almost four years, I have gotten by just fine with a high-deductible insurance policy from Blue Cross.

Before I became self-employed, my family went to the doctor every time there was the slightest illness or complaint. It seemed that the

$25 co-pay was worth it for the peace of mind, but now I am not so sure. After becoming self-employed and realizing that all I could afford was a high-deductible health plan, I started re-evaluating my criteria for doctor visits. Instead of taking my child to the doctor the moment he has a fever or an ear ache, I started waiting a day or so to see if my child began to improve on his own without medical intervention. Medical visits for my family are now mostly preventative in nature. I still routinely receive doctor recommended annual exams and my children have received all the recommended vaccinations. My family and I have adopted a healthy lifestyle that involves eating well and getting regular exercise. The combination of this, along with a good dose of common sense, has eliminated the need for most doctor visits.

Now, I understand that some people have costly medical conditions that limit their options concerning health insurance, but I believe the majority of people can get by with high-deductible insurance plans, assuming they adopt a healthy lifestyle and practice preventative health care.

To supplement the high-deductible plan, self-employed people should also consider enrolling in a Health Savings Account (HSA), which is funded with pre-tax dollars. The money you put into the plan, typically a small monthly premium, can be used towards qualified medical expenses. Currently the maximum yearly contribution for an individual is $3,000; for a family it is $5,950. Often, this is equivalent to your insurance deductible, and you should therefore have your expenses covered. I would suggest you visit the eHealthInsurance web site at https://www.ehealthinsurance.com to learn more about whether a Health Savings Account is right for you.

Bruce Johnson, Partner and Principal Consultant of Toronto-based training and consulting firm, ObjectSharp Consulting

I have had the good fortune to work with Bruce Johnson on two technical certification books for Microsoft Press. Bruce is one of those hard working, salt-of-the-earth kind of guys. He also knows his stuff, especially when it comes to software development and technology in general.

Bruce graduated from the University of Waterloo in Canada with a Bachelor of Science in Mathematics and Computer Science. It was at the University of Waterloo that he discovered how much he loved working with software, especially since the University's innovative co-op program allowed students to alternate between four months in school and four months in an industry job related to their field of study.

After school, Bruce moved to Los Angeles and started a consulting company named TAG Consulting. He operated this business for about 13 years, but in 2002 he and his family decided to move back to Toronto, preferring to raise his children there. Shortly after returning to Toronto, Bruce joined two other consultants and became a partner with ObjectSharp consulting. He has been with this firm ever since and as he says, "I'm absolutely happy with what I do."

> *"One of the things I still love almost twenty years after starting on this path is the freedom that it gives me. On a day-to-day basis, I can decide if I want to go and work or not. I can start earlier or later and end at the corresponding time as the other aspects of my life demand."*

Bruce works hard to stay on top of his field since he realizes that continued learning is critical to success in the software industry. As he told me, "The very rapid turnover of technology means that the ability to remain gainfully employed is very dependent on one's ability to keep pace. This means learning the new tools, techniques, languages, etc that are used on a daily basis. It's not sufficient to become an expert in one area and stay there. Well, to be fair, there are people who do that. But that path was never for me. I never wanted or expected to stay at the same company for 20 years. And if you are going to move around, even as irregularly as 7 or 8 years, you still need to make sure that you remain current."

Even though Bruce is a disciplined person and he works hard at what he does, he also strives to maintain a proper work/life balance that keeps him happy. Money is not the only thing that drives him. He takes pride in doing a good job while simultaneously being paid enough to support his family in a reasonable way. He told me, "I don't consider myself to be wealthy monetarily, but I don't live paycheck to paycheck. And that reduces the level of stress significantly."

Things to Consider

This chapter summary card contains a list of all the items mentioned in this chapter. I suggest you make a copy of this page and paste it up in a place where you will see it every day.

- ❑ **Start-up costs**
- ❑ **Forming a Corporation**
- ❑ **Taxes**
- ❑ **Accounting and Invoices**
- ❑ **Business Insurance**
- ❑ **Health Insurance**

Happiness is not a destination.
It is a method of life.

—Burton Hills

Chapter 8:

Things to Remember

As we come to the end of this book, I wanted to remind you of some things that I feel are important for the self-employed to stay aware of constantly. I also want to let you know how to access the resources mentioned in this book. And finally, I want to tell you about a social web site I am starting which can be used to connect with other people contemplating self-employment.

Expect the unexpected

One thing on which you can depend is that things generally will not turn out the way you planned. It is inevitable that some customer will not pay you, or a product supplier will suddenly go out of business. As in your personal life, things happen in your professional life that are out of your control. The good news is that as a small business owner, you may be better equipped to handle these inconveniences then some of your large competitors. In fact, this agility is one of the most valuable advantages that many small businesses have.

As long as you go into your business mentally and emotionally prepared to expect the unexpected, you should be ok. In addition to this mindset, you need to have the confidence and ability to make big decisions quickly. It may be necessary for you to redefine your product or service offering on very short notice. You need to be prepared to do this and not have to go through an involved, formal process of checking with several other people to confirm. For sole proprietors, this can be very straightforward; for businesses set up as Corporations or Partnerships, it may take more time and discussion. Depending on your personal decision-making preference, you may want to structure your business to let you either make decisions rapidly on your own, or structure it so that others will be involved in the process. Either way, do ensure that you or someone else has been granted the authority to make critical decisions when necessary.

In addition to ensuring you have the authority to make decisions, you need to anticipate what your problems may be. Sit down and draw up a list of what setbacks may occur and then figure out how you would handle them. Roger Arrick told me, "Regularly, I think about what to do when something goes wrong. I consider worst-case scenarios and attempt to prevent them or plan how to deal with them."

Try to think about the things that are not so obvious. For example, what will you do if a sudden large storm knocks out the power to your business for a week? Will it put you out of business? Can you quickly shift your operations to another location? Many businesses do not anticipate events like this and for small businesses, downtime that lasts even just a few days can be quite damaging.

To better anticipate losses that result from natural or man-made disasters, create a game plan and consider buying some kind of disaster insurance. You should also take the time to review the following document produced by the Small Business Administration (http://www.sba.gov/idc/groups/public/documents/sba_homepage/serv_disprep_planningguide.pdf). The document helps you to identify what your potential risks may be and lists suggestions for how to overcome them.

Persistence pays off

Annette Pelliccio told me, "I am very persistent and do not take no for an answer easily." It's a good thing she's made that way, since many small business owners will often hear the word "no" the first time they ask for something. When you are just establishing your business, it is very easy for creditors, vendors, and even customers to assume you will not make it and just write you off.

In the first two years of your business, it is critical that you convince people that your business is here to stay and to demonstrate that the business has a solid foundation to build upon. For example, it may be necessary for you to continue calling a credit card company that has imposed a late fee for a payment which arrived only one day late. The first person you speak to on the phone will likely refuse to waive the fee. But, if you are persistent and keep calling back or, better yet, speak to the supervisor, you may be surprised to find that you only have to ask the right person to get the answer you want.

To help you get around an initial "no," remember to remain calm and never shout at anyone. No one is going to give you anything if you start yelling at them. Stay focused on your goal of getting a yes, or even just a maybe. Remain positive, even when the person you are talking to starts to behave negatively. People are much more likely to give you things if they feel you are optimistic.

If the person you have contacted refuses to give in and you are not getting the response you want even after escalating the problem, step back and re-evaluate. Sometimes when you get too close to something, you cannot see it for what it really is. You may need to adopt an entirely new strategy. For example, if a potential customer keeps telling you that you just don't have enough experience, consider offering them an option of providing your service for a discount or even for free. Now, be careful not to give too much away, but you may have to sacrifice in the short term to reap rewards in the long term.

In today's fast paced society, it is easy to get wrapped up in the hit or miss strategy that many companies adopt. We would rather try a thousand things and get them all wrong, then just buckle down and focus on one thing at a time. Sometimes, it may be necessary for you to stick with something until you get the answer you need. The trick is learning when to hang in there and when to move on. Until you get the hang of this, try to avoid any extreme reactions, such as giving up after the first try, or hounding someone unreasonably.

Focus on building a good reputation

Mark Dunn told me that he will do whatever it takes to deliver for his customers, even when that costs him considerably in terms of the time and effort expended. He takes his reputation very seriously and he strives to treat everyone with respect. Mark is grateful to live in a country where he can fulfill his dreams, but he does not take that for granted. He told me, "I think the main keys to achieving your dreams are building a great reputation, showing up and getting the work done, focusing on long term goals rather than short term profits, making sure you work with good people and taking care of the people you work with. If you can do those things, you'll have a leg up on most of your competition."

I agree with Mark and think that it is very important to always take the high road, not only in your professional life, but your personal life as well. I include your personal life because I believe it is impossible to be truthful and respectful to others in your professional life if you cannot do the same in your personal life.

Sometimes it can be hard to do the "right thing", but generally we all know what the right thing is. When faced with an ethical or moral decision in your business or personal life, carefully consider the consequences of taking the easy way out. Once you establish a business, you are essentially creating a legacy that may live on for many years. It is possible your business could be passed on to your children, a spouse, or even a friend. You want to make sure you pass on something that is of the highest value and integrity.

The American Dream

America was founded on the premise that all men and women are created equal and that everyone deserves an opportunity to pursue happiness. I believe the spirit and enthusiasm that created this great nation still exists today. If anything, it may be stronger. There is nowhere else in the world where you have as many opportunities to succeed and lead a peaceful and happy life.

Despite the recession and the war in Iraq, we live in very good times. Technical innovations have brought enormous advantages to our society in the last few decades and the possibilities for future advancements are almost limitless. Additionally, the current global recession may actually serve as an advantage to individual small business owners since many large competitors have been removed due to the economic strain.

I completely agree with Mark Dunn when he said that, "I'm grateful to live in a country where anyone can hang out a shingle, start a business and achieve their dreams". We are all very lucky and this is the best time for you to realize your share of the "American Dream".

In the next section, you will learn about a gentleman that personifies the American dream. Roger Arrick is one of those individuals who prove that you can overcome any obstacle if you are driven and love what you do.

Roger Arrick: Owner of Arrick Robotics

Despite the fact that his father warned him that a person couldn't make a good living without a degree, Roger Arrick took a chance, left college early and started his own computer products company in 1980. Since then Roger has transformed his primary business into a robotics company (Arrick Robotics), started two more businesses, and written a book titled, "Robot Building for Dummies". Not bad, considering he was operating in a business environment that underwent recessions and the big "dot-com" bust; economic events that brought down many businesses started by the brightest minds from Ivy League schools.

But Roger is not the type of guy to let a few challenges get in his way. As he puts it, "What I lack in intelligence, I make up for with stubbornness. And, it takes plenty of stubbornness." But Roger has more than stubbornness on his side. He has developed a keen ability to think outside the box and to look for unique solutions to design problems. "It's very discouraging for me to have an idea then learn that someone else in another place and time did the same thing," says Roger.

> *Passion is more important than intelligence and money. Wisdom is more valuable than intelligence, and acquaintances more important than money."*

Roger's web site, http://www.arrickrobotics.com offers a mobile robot called the ARobot which can be used by educators and hobbyists to better understand how a robot is built and operates. Along with his book, "Robot Building for Dummies", which details how to assemble and enhance the ARobot, future generations of roboticists will take their first steps in gathering the skills needed to work in the fast growing robotics industry.

Roger works hard to keep his businesses active and he estimates that most of his time is spent focused on the details of running a business. Even though he works hard, Roger has learned the importance of seeking a balanced lifestyle. He strives to eat right and always get a good night's sleep. He told me, "It's common for entrepreneurs to burn the midnight oil and run on caffeine. I think this is an unhealthy, unbalanced way to live and ultimately sabotages a person's ambition, mind and body. If you can do something great, it's of little use if you can only do it for a short time." It's a good thing Roger thinks this way, since the growing number of people now interested in robotics will no doubt be depending on Roger for years to come.

Join the No Limits community

If you have gotten this far in the book, there is a good chance that you enjoyed it and hopefully you are inspired to make the jump towards self-employment. Writing this book has been a lot of fun for me and I would very much like to continue to inspire and educate others on the terrific opportunities that self-employment offers. Therefore, I have set up a social networking web site that can be accessed by fans of this book.

You can access the web site through the following URL: http://nolimitsthebook.ning.com/. I plan on blogging regularly, but anyone can join as a member and start blogging as well. The web site also includes a forum that can be used to start a discussion among members. I hope you will consider joining and participating in this online social community. I look forward to meeting you there.

Access links from the NoLimitsTheBook web site

In addition to the social web site, I have set up a web site dedicated exclusively to the book. On this site you can access sample chapters, order copies of the book, and also access links mentioned in each of the chapters. The web site will also include errata for this edition of the book. You can access the web site through the following URL: http://www.nolimitsthebook.com.

Things to Remember

This chapter summary card contains a list of all the items mentioned in this chapter. I suggest you make a copy of this page and paste it up in a place where you will see it every day.

- ❑ **Expect the Unexpected**
- ❑ **Persistence Pays Off**
- ❑ **Focus on Building a Good Reputation**
- ❑ **The American Dream**
- ❑ **Join the No Limits Community**
  http://nolimitsthebook.ning.com
- ❑ **Access Resources from the No Limits Web Site**
  http://www.nolimitsthebook.com

Biographies

✧ **Mark Dunn, President and Owner of DUNN Training and Consulting**

Mark Dunn has over 20 years of experience in the disciplines of software engineering, database administration, and project management. For the past three years, Mark has been awarded MVP status for his contributions to the Visual Studio .Net community and he serves as Microsoft's Regional Director covering the Southeast United States. Mark also co-founded .Net Rocks, an Internet radio program for .Net developers recognized in over 80 countries and now hosted by Microsoft on the MSDN site. Mark is also a Microsoft Certified Trainer, Application Developer, Solution Developer for .Net, and Database Administrator.

✧ **Annette Pelliccio, Founder and CEO, The Happy Gardener, Inc**

Annette Pelliccio is a third generation garden business owner with a passion for educating home gardeners and communities on healthy alternatives to conventional garden and lawn care practices. She has developed a line of organic plant foods, soil conditioners and lawn care designed for easy and economical organic gardening. Annette and her nationwide team of distributors educate on organics and how to participate in the Plant a Row for the Hungry campaign.

✧ **Chellie Campbell, Creator of the Financial Stress Reduction workshops and author of *The Wealthy Spirit* and *Zero to Zillionaire***

Creator of the popular Financial Stress Reduction® Workshops which now has licensed Coaches throughout the country, Chellie Campbell's first book was The Wealthy Spirit: Daily Affirmations for Financial Stress Reduction (Sourcebooks, 2002) which was chosen as a Book-of-the-Week on the Dr. Laura Schlessinger radio show and a GlobalNet Book-of-the-Month selection. Her publisher asked her to write her second book, Zero to Zillionaire: 8 Foolproof Steps to Financial Peace of Mind, which was released by Sourcebooks in April, 2006. You can find out more about Chellie on her web site at chellie.com.

✧ **Joan M. Roberts, Certified Career Management Coach and owner of CareerCounseling.com**

Joan M. Roberts, MA, CAGS opened CareerMasters in 1992 to assist professionals with their career needs. In 1995 CareerMasters expanded to include CareerCounseling.com. CareerMasters and CareerCounseling.com provide corporate outplacement, career assessment, resume development, career coaching and Myers-Briggs (MBTI) services. Joan is a Certified Career Management Coach, a Certified Professional Resume Writer and a Certified MBTI Practitioner. Several of Joan's resumes have been published in national and international publications, including "Resumes for Executives, Managers and Other Administrators" "Professional Resumes for Accounting, Tax, Finance, and Law", and "America's

Top Resumes for America's Top Jobs". She has helped hundreds of professionals regain a sense of clarity, balance and momentum in their lives

Joan is a graduate of the University of Notre Dame with a BA degree in Psychology and a graduate of American International College with an MA degree and a Certificate of Advanced Graduate Study (CAGS) in Human Resource Development. In the community, Joan has served on the board of the Ronald McDonald House; as President of the Notre Dame Club of Maine; and a founding board member of the Maine Affiliate of the Susan G. Komen Breast Cancer Foundation.

✧ Alex V. Cook, Independent Software Developer, freelance music journalist and author of *Darkness, Racket* and *Twang*

Alex V. Cook is a software developer, family man, as well as a food and music critic living and working in Baton Rouge. His writing has appeared in the Oxford American, the Believer, DownBeat, the Wire and others. He is the music editor for outsideleft.com and his first book Darkness, Racket, and Twang was published in 2006 by SideCartel, for whom he is feverishly working on a second. The full effect of his obsessive mind can be felt at alexvcook.com.

✧ Bruce Johnson, Partner, Principal Consultant with ObjectSharp Consulting

Bruce Johnson is a Principal Consultant with ObjectSharp and a 25-year veteran of the computer industry. He spent half of that time working in the MultiValue database and UNIX marketplace, but the past 14 years have been spent on projects at the leading edge of Windows technology, including using .NET since the introduction of version 1.0. His experience includes the creation of commercial web applications using AJAX, the implementation of Web Services in a financial institution and the building of various Windows-based applications for software vendors. As well as his experience in system design and development, he has also given over 200 presentations at user conferences all over North America and has been published in International Spectrum magazine (where he had a column for six years), ASPToday.com and C#Today.com. He is also the co-author of *The ASP 3.0 Code Maintenance handbook* (Wrox Press)

✧ Roger Arrick, Owner of Arrick Robotics

Roger Arrick is owner of Arrick Robotics, a small company he founded in 1987 where he designs and manufactures positioning systems for industry and mobile robots for hobbyists and educators. He also runs synthesizers.com, a maker of vintage-style sound synthesis products for music production. Roger also enjoys several hobbies including genealogy research, playing drums, and walking his retired racing greyhound. Roger and his family live in the piney woods of east Texas near Tyler.

Glossary

AIM Mail

Free web-based e-mail account available from America Online (AOL). The account currently offers unlimited storage space and e-mails can be accessed from a mobile device. If you are interested in obtaining a free account from AOL, you should visit http://www.aol.com and click the "Get Free Mail" button.

Bing

Web-based search provider created by Microsoft and released in June of 2009. Microsoft claims that the search engine, accessible through the following URL, http://www.bing.com, acts more like a decision engine and can also help consumers to book travel flights, find hotels, learn about your health and even locate local information such as which freeway you should use when driving to work.

Certified Public Accountant (CPA)

Statutory title given to accountants in the United States who have passed the Uniform Certified Public Accountant Examination and have met additional state specific requirements concerning education and experience.

COBOL

Acronym for COmmon Business-Oriented Language, this is one of the oldest programming languages created in 1959 by Grace Hopper.

Originally a procedural-based language, in 2002 a standard was developed to support the modern feature known as object-oriented programming.

Databases

Term used to describe an electronic set of data records that are stored on some type of computer system. A common database type is a relational database, in which data records are grouped using common attributes, thus allowing them to be organized easier. The database is then managed by software known as a Relational Database Management System (RDMS). Two of the most popular RDMS's on the market today are Microsoft SQL Server and Oracle Database.

Deductible

In the case of health insurance, this represents an agreed upon portion of money that must be paid by a health insurance policy holder before the Insurance company will cover any additional qualified medical expenses.

Desktop Client

Term used to refer to computer software that executes locally on a user's desktop machine. This is typically used to distinguish software that runs locally and must first be fully downloaded and installed on a user machine as opposed to software that is executed on a Web Server using an Internet connection.

Domain Name

Identification label typically used to distinguish a web site available on the World Wide Web. The domain name is registered with a domain name registrar, which is a company accredited by the International Corporation for Assigned Names and Numbers (ICANN). The name is used to uniquely identify an Internet host computer which contains the target web site.

Gmail

Free web-based e-mail account offered by Google. The account offers a spam filter to keep junk mail out of your inbox, over 7GB of storage space and mobile access. If you are interested in obtaining a free account from Google, you should visit http:///www.google.com and click the "Mail" link located in the upper left-hand corner of the page. From there you can click the "Create an Account" button.

Health Savings Account (HSA)

Individually owned savings account which can be used by people who have a high-deductible health plan to pay for qualified medical expenses. Funds deposited into the account are not subject to federal income tax.

High-Deductible Health Plan

Type of health insurance plan which offers lower premiums and higher deductibles than traditional health insurance plans.

Internet

Represents a global network of private and public computers that are all connected and utilize a common and standardized way of communicating. The protocols that connect all these computers are known as Transmission Control Protocol and Internet Protocol, or TCP/IP.

Microsoft Live Mail

Free web-based e-mail account from Microsoft. Includes access to a calendar, event reminders and can even be accessed when you are not connected to the Internet. Like Gmail, it also includes a powerful spam filter to keep unwanted messages out of your inbox. If you are interested in obtaining a free account, go to http://home.live.com and click the "Sign Up" button.

Microsoft Outlook

Desktop client software from Microsoft which acts as a personal information manager. The software is part of an application suite, or a collection of related software, known as Microsoft Office suite. It can be used to view and manage e-mail messages on the local desktop machine and includes a calendar, task manager, contact manager, note taking, and a journal.

Premiums

In the case of health insurance, this represents the amount of money charged to a policy holder in exchange for insurance coverage.

Search Engine Optimization (SEO)

Process of increasing the number of visits to a web site via search engines such as Google or Bing. These visits come about when a user submits a keyword search word(s) to a search engine, lists the results, and then clicks one of the search result links to visit the web site. The primary objective of the SEO process is to ensure that the target web site is listed in the first page and near the top of the resulting search results.

Storage Space

In terms of e-mail, storage space represents the amount of hard disk storage available for storing e-mail messages. The larger the hard disk, the higher the number of e-mails that can be preserved.

Yahoo Mail

Free web-based e-mail account from Yahoo. This account offers unlimited storage, access from a mobile device and spam and virus protection. If you are interested in obtaining a free account, go to http://mail.yahoo.com and click on the Sign Up for Yahoo" button.

References

Bergman, Mike "Press Release: Nation Adds 1 Million Self-Employed Businesses to Reach 18.6 Million, Census Bureau Reports", September 30, 2005; U.S. Census Bureau News, http://www.census.gov/Press-Release/www/releases/archives/business_ownership/005784.html

Brew, Alex "Press Release: Trusting your instincts leads you to the right answer" January 8, 2007; University College London, http://www.eurekalert.org/pub_releases/2007-01/ucl-tyi010807.php

Chatzky, Jean "Don't let money woes get the best of you" August 18, 2008; NBC News - http://www.chellie.com/press_today.html

Cox, Michael & Alm, Richard "You are what you spend" February 10, 2008; New York Times, http://www.nytimes.com/2008/02/10/opinion/10cox.html?_r=3&th&emc=th&oref=slogin&oref=slogin/

Internal Revenue Service "Self-Employment Tax" United States Department of the Treasury - http://www.irs.gov/businesses/small/article/0,,id=98846,00.html

Inspirational Quotes from HeartsAndMinds.org - http://www.heartsandminds.org/quotes/quotes.htm

Lee, Maggie "Feature Interview: Healer of Money Disorders, Spending Bulimia and Income Anorexia - Chellie Campbell" New LadderToSuccess.com - http://www.chellie.com/press_nlts.html

Mayo Clinic Staff "Positive thinking: Reduce Stress, enjoy life more" MayoClinic.com, http://www.mayoclinic.com/health/positive-thinking/SR00009

Mould, Chrissie "S Corp vs. LLC: Which structure if Right for Your Business" PowerHomeBiz.com - http://www.irs.gov/businesses/small/article/0,,id=98846,00.html

National Science Foundation "Employed females 16 years and older, by detailed occupation: Selected years, 1983-2007 annual averages" http://www.nsf.gov/statistics/wmpd/pdf/tabh-2.pdf

Pelliccio, Annette "Our Story"; TheHappyGardener.info, http://www.thehappygardener.info/index.php?getpage=101

Perez, William "Types of Business Organizations" June 12, 2009; About.com - http://taxes.about.com/od/taxplanning/a/incorporating_2.htm

United States Census Bureau "Credit Cards – Holders, Number, Spending and Debt, 2000 and 2006, and Projections, 2010" http://marketplace.publicradio.org/pdf/credit_cards_census.pdf

Index

F

G

H

I

Quick Order Form

Fax Order: 225-635-5510. Send this form.

Telephone Order: Call 1-877-285-5509 toll-free. Have your credit card ready.

Email Order: orders@custsolutions.net. Include all information from this form.

Postal Order: Custom Solutions, Order Department, 5559 Hilltop Circle, Saint Francisville, LA 70775, USA. Telephone: 225-635-5509

Please send me ____ copies of *No Limits: How I escaped the clutches of Corporate America to live the self-employed life of my dreams* (First Edition).

Name: ______________________________

Address: ______________________________

City: ____________________ State: __________ Zip: __________

Telephone: ______________________________

Email Address: ______________________________

Credit Card Number: ______________________________

Expiration Date: (month) ________ (year) ________

Last three digits, on back of card ________

Signature: ______________________________

Note: If sending a check, make check out to **Custom Solutions, LLC** and the amount should be **$16.95** per book + **$4.00** for shipping and handling + **9%** sales tax if shipping to an address within the State of Louisiana.

If you have an International order, please email us your information and we will let you know if shipment to that country is possible, along with the cost.

Quick Order Form

Fax Order:	225-635-5510. Send this form.
Telephone Order:	Call 1-877-285-5509 toll-free. Have your credit card ready.
Email Order:	orders@custsolutions.net. Include all information from this form.
Postal Order:	Custom Solutions, Order Department, 5559 Hilltop Circle, Saint Francisville, LA 70775, USA. Telephone: 225-635-5509

Please send me ____ copies of *No Limits: How I escaped the clutches of Corporate America to live the self-employed life of my dreams* (First Edition).

Name: ______________________________

Address: ______________________________

City: ____________________ State: __________ Zip: __________

Telephone: ______________________________

Email Address: ______________________________

Credit Card Number: ______________________________

Expiration Date: (month) ________ (year) ________

Last three digits, on back of card ________

Signature: ______________________________

Note: If sending a check, make check out to **Custom Solutions, LLC** and the amount should be **$16.95** per book + **$4.00** for shipping and handling + **9%** sales tax if shipping to an address within the State of Louisiana.

If you have an International order, please email us your information and we will let you know if shipment to that country is possible, along with the cost.

Quick Order Form

Fax Order: 225-635-5510. Send this form.

Telephone Order: Call 1-877-285-5509 toll-free. Have your credit card ready.

Email Order: orders@custsolutions.net. Include all information from this form.

Postal Order: Custom Solutions, Order Department, 5559 Hilltop Circle, Saint Francisville, LA 70775, USA. Telephone: 225-635-5509

Please send me ____ copies of *No Limits: How I escaped the clutches of Corporate America to live the self-employed life of my dreams* (First Edition).

Name: ______________________________

Address: ______________________________

City: ____________________ State: __________ Zip: __________

Telephone: ______________________________

Email Address: ______________________________

Credit Card Number: ______________________________

Expiration Date: (month) ________ (year) ________

Last three digits, on back of card ________

Signature: ______________________________

Note: If sending a check, make check out to **Custom Solutions, LLC** and the amount should be **$16.95** per book + **$4.00** for shipping and handling + **9%** sales tax if shipping to an address within the State of Louisiana.

If you have an International order, please email us your information and we will let you know if shipment to that country is possible, along with the cost.

Quick Order Form

Fax Order: 225-635-5510. Send this form.

Telephone Order: Call 1-877-285-5509 toll-free. Have your credit card ready.

Email Order: orders@custsolutions.net. Include all information from this form.

Postal Order: Custom Solutions, Order Department, 5559 Hilltop Circle, Saint Francisville, LA 70775, USA. Telephone: 225-635-5509

Please send me ____ copies of *No Limits: How I escaped the clutches of Corporate America to live the self-employed life of my dreams* (First Edition).

Name: ______________________________

Address: ______________________________

City: ____________________ State: __________ Zip: __________

Telephone: ______________________________

Email Address: ______________________________

Credit Card Number: ______________________________

Expiration Date: (month) ________ (year) ________

Last three digits, on back of card ________

Signature: ______________________________

Note: If sending a check, make check out to **Custom Solutions, LLC** and the amount should be **$16.95** per book + **$4.00** for shipping and handling + **9%** sales tax if shipping to an address within the State of Louisiana.

If you have an International order, please email us your information and we will let you know if shipment to that country is possible, along with the cost.

Quick Order Form

Fax Order: 225-635-5510. Send this form.

Telephone Order: Call 1-877-285-5509 toll-free. Have your credit card ready.

Email Order: orders@custsolutions.net. Include all information from this form.

Postal Order: Custom Solutions, Order Department, 5559 Hilltop Circle, Saint Francisville, LA 70775, USA. Telephone: 225-635-5509

Please send me ____ copies of *No Limits: How I escaped the clutches of Corporate America to live the self-employed life of my dreams* (First Edition).

Name: ____

Address: ____

City:______________________ State:__________ Zip: __________

Telephone: ____

Email Address: _______________________________________

Credit Card Number:____________________________________

Expiration Date: (month) ________ (year) ________

Last three digits, on back of card ________

Signature: ____

Note: If sending a check, make check out to **Custom Solutions, LLC** and the amount should be **$16.95** per book + **$4.00** for shipping and handling + **9%** sales tax if shipping to an address within the State of Louisiana.

If you have an International order, please email us your information and we will let you know if shipment to that country is possible, along with the cost.